The Growing in Faith Bible Storybook

English Standard Version®

Our special thanks to artist Lon Eric Craven, who brought the story of God's love to life in his beautiful artwork accompanying the 125 Bible narratives.

CONCORDIA PUBLISHING HOUSE · SAINT LOUIS

Copyright © 2019 Concordia Publishing House
3558 S. Jefferson Ave., St. Louis, MO 63118-3968
1-800-325-3040 • cph.org

Text © 2018 Concordia Publishing House

Illustrations by Lon Eric Craven © 2018 Concordia Publishing House

Manufactured in East Peoria, IL/063692/416335

2   3   4   5   6   7   8   9   10   11   31   30   29   28   27   26   25   24   23   22

Table of Contents

OLD TESTAMENT

JESUS' BIRTH

JESUS' MINISTRY

NEW TESTAMENT

Introduction

Story time has a special place in every child's life. It has particular impact when that time includes Bible stories, because through them, parents and children are drawn closer in their shared faith and—most important—closer to their Savior.

Bible literacy begins early, as children become familiar with words, people, places, events, and concepts. Hearing stories at a young age about God's people builds intimacy with the Scriptures and their application to everyday life. Reading Bible stories with children helps them understand that

- the Bible is God's true Word to us;
- God is active in every aspect of our lives;
- God uses His power for our benefit; and
- God keeps His promises.

This collection of retold biblical events is compiled especially for families with children ages 3 and up. It demonstrates that every story in the Bible has a purpose, whether to show us God in creation or to teach us how to live in relation to Him and to others. The narratives are written to encourage understanding of how God loves, forgives, guides, and protects us. And they are presented in readable language so children will listen, comprehend, and remember.

The Growing in Faith Bible Storybook is interactive. Each narrative begins with a question to encourage the hearer to think and apply Christian concepts and continues by explaining why the story is important and what it means to us today. Narratives conclude with a prayer to help children develop the practice of regular, earnest, and confident conversation with their Lord and to engage families in praying together.

The narratives are accompanied by historically accurate illustrations rendered in vivid colors, which stimulate the imagination, expand on the Bible stories, and further understanding. These realistic illustrations indicate to children that the people, places, and events in Bible stories were real. Therefore, learning takes place on multiple levels as children hear and see and discuss. And as understanding increases, faith is nurtured, by the power of the Holy Spirit.

Parents, grandparents, caregivers, and educators can trust this collection to communicate the truth of God's Word for His people. The narratives are true to God's Word and preserve the facts of the unified account of man in his relationship to God.

Most important, every story points to our Lord Jesus, Redeemer and Savior, true man and true God, who is the source of our hope and reason for our joy.

The
OLD TESTAMENT

God Creates the World

Where is your favorite outside place?

God made the mountains, hills, rivers, and lakes. He made the forests and grassland. He made trees and flowers. He made birds, fish, cats, and dogs. Let's talk about how He made them.

In the beginning, there was only God. Nothing else. Then God spoke, and suddenly the heavens and the earth were here. But the earth was covered with water, and darkness was everywhere. So God said, "Let there be light." And immediately, light appeared. God separated the light from the darkness so that each day there will be time for darkness and time for light. God called the time of light Day, and He called the time of darkness Night. This was the first day.

The second day, God said, "Let there be an expanse in the midst of the waters." Some water moved up above, and some moved down below and left a space behind. God called that new space Sky.

On the third day, God said, "Let the waters under the heavens be gathered together into one place so the dry ground can appear." God called the waters Seas, and He called the dry land Earth. But the land was bare and empty. So God spoke, and all kinds of plants grew out of the land—fruit trees, leafy shade trees, pretty flowering trees, and evergreen trees. Bushes, vines, and prairie grass appeared. God made tulips, roses, and lush, green grass.

On the fourth day, God said, "Let there be lights in the sky to separate the day from the night." So He made the sun to light up the day. He made the moon and stars to light the night.

On the fifth day, God said, "Let the waters be filled with living creatures, and let birds fly above the earth across the sky." All kinds of fish appeared—great and small. God also made whales and dolphins to play in the oceans, and He filled the rivers and lakes with all kinds of fish. He filled the sky with all kinds of birds—sparrows, robins, cardinals, owls, hawks, and eagles.

On the sixth day, God said, "Let the earth bring forth living creatures." He made wild beasts like lions, elephants, and zebras; livestock like horses, cows, and pigs; and crawling things like worms, spiders, and ants.

Then last of all, God said, "Let us make humans in Our image." So God made a man and a woman. Since they were made in God's image, they were able to know God. They could love Him and talk to Him. And just like God, they were good, caring, and kind.

God looked at everything He made, and He said that it was very good. Then on the seventh day, God stopped creating things and rested.

So one day each week, we stop and rest. We come to church and Sunday School to thank Him for creating us, to talk about all the things He does to take care of us, and to remember all the good gifts He gives to us.

LET'S PRAY: Heavenly Father, You made such a wonderful world, and You made me too. Thank You for sending Your own Son, Jesus, to save me. Amen.

God Creates Adam and Eve Genesis 2

What do you like most about your best friend?

God made humans to be together. We see that when God made the first man and woman. Here is their story.

Have you ever made anything out of play dough or clay? When God made the first person, He reached down into the ground and took a big glob of dirt and clay. He carefully formed the man's body. He shaped his head, eyes, ears, nose, and mouth. He molded his shoulders and arms, hands, and fingers. He formed his legs, feet, and toes.

Then God breathed into the man's nose. And God's breath made the man come alive. He opened his eyes, stood up on his feet, and looked at the beautiful world around him. Because he was formed out of the ground, God called his name Adam, which means "dirt" or "ground."

But God knew it was not good for the man to be alone. He wanted Adam to know it too. So He brought every kind of animal to him. Adam studied each animal carefully and gave it just the right name. He loved all the animals, but something was missing. None of them could really be the kind of friend Adam needed—not even a dog or a horse.

So God made the man fall deep asleep. The Lord wanted all people to be connected together, so He took a rib out of Adam's side while he slept. God formed dirt and clay around that rib to make a woman who would be the perfect friend for Adam. The Lord breathed His breath into the woman, and she became alive too, just like Adam. God woke up Adam and brought the woman to him. Then He married them together as husband and wife.

Adam was very happy because he finally had a friend who was like him, but different too. They could talk together, laugh together, and make plans together. Adam named her Eve because she would become the mother of the human family.

And that is how all of us people are connected together. Eve came from Adam, and all of us come from Adam and Eve. We may look different, dress different, and sound different, but we are all Adam and Eve's children. Even more than that, since God made Adam and Eve in His own image, He has made each of us special, able to know and love Him as He comes to us and shows Himself to us.

It was not good for Adam to be alone. And it is not good for you and me to be alone either. That is why God gives us parents, family, and friends. He wants us to love and care for one another. He cares so much He sent His only Son, Jesus, to become a little baby born of Mary—to be our Brother and our Savior.

LET'S PRAY: Holy Father, it is not good to be alone. Thank You for giving us parents who love us, family members who care for us, and friends who make our lives so much better. Most of all, thank You for sending Your own Son, Jesus Christ, who loved us and died to save us. In Jesus' name. Amen.

Sin Enters the World

Genesis 3

Describe a time someone tried to get you to do something you knew was wrong.

Adam and Eve lived in the Garden of Eden and took care of it. It was full of fruit they could eat whenever they were hungry. But God told Adam not to eat from the tree of the knowledge of good and evil. If he ate its fruit, he would die.

Then the devil came and took control of a serpent. He asked Eve if God really said not to eat from any tree in the garden. She told him they could eat from every tree but the tree of the knowledge of good and evil; if they ate it, or even touched it, they would die.

The serpent hissed, "You will not surely die." He promised that she would become like God if she ate its fruit.

Adam was with Eve. He knew the serpent was lying, but Eve believed him. She thought the fruit looked beautiful. But best of all, it would make her like God. So she grabbed one. Adam knew the serpent was lying to Eve (see 1 Timothy 2:14), but he ate the fruit she handed him, knowing he would die.

But the fruit did not make them wise; it only made them feel terrible. For the first time, they knew they were naked. They thought this horrible feeling might go away if they covered their bodies with leaves. Then they heard a terrible, scary sound—God walking toward them! Shaking in fear, Adam and Eve tried to hide deep in the garden. But it was no use—you can never hide from God.

The Lord asked Adam, "Where are you?"

Adam answered, "I heard the sound of You in the garden, and I was afraid because I was naked, and I hid myself." God asked how he knew he was naked. Then God asked Adam if he ate the fruit He had told him not to eat. Adam blamed Eve.

God asked the woman, "What is this that you have done?" Eve answered, "The serpent deceived me, and I ate." Too late, Eve knew the serpent's promise was an empty lie.

God told the serpent one of Eve's children would destroy him: "He shall bruise your head, and you shall bruise His heel." Jesus was that child. On the cross, He suffered and died, but He destroyed Satan's power and gave eternal life to all who believe in Him.

Next, God told Adam and Eve they had to leave the garden and grow food in the fields outside. But God went with them. Adam and Eve told their children and grandchildren about God's promise to save us.

Adam and Eve changed when they ate that fruit; we were changed too. Our hearts and minds are turned against God. We do bad things and don't do the good things God wants us to do. But the Lord sent Jesus to save us, and He destroyed the power of sin and the devil.

LET'S PRAY: God, our Father, thank You for sending Jesus to save Adam and Eve and all of us. Help me treat others kindly and tell them about Your promise. In Jesus' name. Amen.

Cain and Abel

Describe a time you were really, really angry at someone.

Adam and Eve had a baby boy and named him Cain. He grew up to be a farmer. They had another baby boy and called him Abel. He grew up to be a shepherd. Adam and Eve taught their sons God's promise to send a Savior. To thank God for that great promise, they burned up some of their food with fire. We call that an offering.

When Cain and Abel grew up, the time came to bring their offering. Cain was not very happy; he didn't want to give up some of his food. But Abel brought the very best he had because he loved God and knew how much he needed the Savior God promised. God was pleased with Abel's sacrifice, but not with Cain's. That made Cain really, really mad.

But Cain should have been mad at himself, not at Abel. He should have realized how much he needed the Savior and asked God to forgive him and help him do better next time. Instead, he hated his brother Abel for making him look bad.

God talked to Cain. He warned Cain about the anger burning in his heart. That anger wanted to take control and make him do something bad. But Cain didn't listen. Instead, he led Abel out into a field, and then hit him so hard he died.

Afterward, the Lord asked Cain, "Where is Abel your brother?" Cain didn't feel bad at all. He said, "Am I my brother's keeper?" Was God expecting him to follow Abel around like he was still a little boy? But God knew. He asked him, "What have you done? The voice of your brother's blood is crying to Me from the ground." God loves each of us very much, and when one of us gets hurt, God does something about it.

God told Cain no crops would grow for him anymore. Cain should have felt bad about what he did to Abel, but instead he only felt sorry for himself. "My punishment is greater than I can bear." He had just killed his brother—but he thought God was the one being unfair. He was afraid his other brothers would punish him for killing their brother Abel.

But God still loved Cain. He put a mark on him so when his brothers would see that mark, they would leave him alone. Cain should have thanked God for that mark. He should have begged God to send the Savior to forgive him for killing Abel. Instead, Cain wanted nothing more to do with God. He turned and went away to live his life without God.

Sometimes we get really angry at people. When we pray to God to help us, He takes that anger away from our hearts and fills us with love for them instead.

LET'S PRAY: God, You know the times I have been really angry at people. Sometimes it was because of bad things they did to me. Other times I was angry for no good reason at all. Please forgive me of all sinful anger, for the sake of Jesus. Teach me to love everyone around me the way You love me. In Jesus' name. Amen.

Noah Builds the Ark

What scares you most about storms?

God promised one of Adam and Eve's sons would be next in the line that led to His promised Savior. But which son? Cain turned away from God and left. Abel was killed by Cain before he had any children. God chose another son, Seth, to be next in line.

When Seth grew up, he had a son, and the line continued from father to son, on and on. Seth's family kept telling their sons and daughters about God's promise. Many years later, a son named Noah was born. His parents taught him about God's promise, and Noah believed.

But most of Seth's family didn't know God; they didn't care about His love or His promises. Like Cain and his family, they did whatever they wanted and didn't care whom they hurt. God felt deep sorrow when He saw how badly people treated one another. He wished He had never made humans. So He decided to send a huge, terrible flood of water to wash away every person from the earth. But then He looked at Noah.

Noah was not a perfect person. Like you and me, Noah did bad things he shouldn't, and he didn't always do the good things God wanted him to do. But Noah was sorry for his sins and trusted God's promise to send His Son to take his sins away.

God loved Noah and warned him about the flood He planned to send. He showed him how to build a huge ship called an ark to save Noah and his family from the flood. Noah's ark was three stories tall. He built a huge door on the side where the animals came in. He left a small gap between the walls and roof along the top to let light inside.

Noah's neighbors asked what he was building. Noah warned them about the coming flood. He said they needed to ask God to forgive them for the bad things they did and trust His promise to save them through His Son. But they laughed at him.

After many years, it was done. God brought all kinds of land animals to the ark to keep them alive. Noah took them into the ark with all the food they would need. God closed the ark's door.

Then the flood came. Water shot up in giant fountains from deep below the ground and under the seas. Rain poured down from the clouds. The waters lifted the ark high above the ground. The waters kept rising until they covered all the land—even the highest mountains. All the people and land animals outside the ark were killed, and only Noah and his family were safe—eight people living together and taking care of all the animals in the ark.

Storms can be very scary. Lightning flashes so bright it hurts our eyes, and thunder is so loud it shakes our house. But Jesus is stronger than the storms, and He always watches over us.

LET'S PRAY: Lord God, our Father, thank You for saving Noah and his family in the ark. Help us to believe Your promises like Noah did and to share Jesus' love with the people who don't know Him. In Jesus' name. Amen.

God's Promise to Noah

Describe what it feels like to walk across your yard after a long rainstorm.

For forty days, the rain poured heavily on the roof of the ark. Every human and land animal outside the ark died. But inside the ark, Noah, his family, and all the animals were safe and dry.

Finally, after forty days, the rain stopped. But floodwaters don't go away the minute the rain stops. It's like a bathtub full of water. The water doesn't start going down just because we turn off the faucet; we have to open the drain. And even when we open the drain, the water doesn't disappear immediately. It takes time for all the water to run down through the drain.

That's how it was with Noah's flood. The rains stopped after forty days, but the waters stayed high for 150 days. Then God remembered Noah. He made a wind blow over the earth, and the waters started draining off the land very, very slowly.

In the seventh month after the flood started, on the seventeenth day of the month, Noah's ark landed high on a mountain in a place called Ararat (AIR-uh-rat). But it was still way too early to leave the ark. The ground had to dry out, and plants had to start growing again so the animals would have food to eat.

Noah waited forty more days, and then he opened the ark's window. He sent out a raven. It flew back and forth over the earth until the waters dried up. He also sent a dove. But the dove came back to the ark because it couldn't find a dry place to land.

After seven days, Noah sent out the dove again. This time it came back carrying a leaf it plucked from an olive tree. Noah knew the plants were growing and the animals would soon have enough food to eat.

After seven more days, Noah sent the dove off again. This time, it didn't return—the ground was dry. Finally, a year and ten days after the flood started, God told Noah and his family to go out from the ark, have many children, and begin filling the earth again.

Noah was very thankful, so he made an offering to God. God smelled the sweet smoke and was pleased with Noah's faith. He made a promise to Noah, his family, and all land animals that He would never destroy the world with a flood again. And God uses the rainbow to remind us of that great promise.

In the morning or evening when a rainstorm is passing, you can often see a rainbow in the sky. When you do, remember God's promise to protect us. And remember the cross where Jesus suffered and died. That's where God kept His promise to forgive our sins and save us from death.

LET'S PRAY: Holy Lord God, thank You for Your rainbow. It reminds us of Your promise to never again send a flood to destroy the world. Thank You most of all for keeping Your promise to send Your Son, Jesus, who died on the cross to save us and let us live with You forever. In Jesus' name. Amen.

The Tower of Babel

If you could learn any language in the world, which language would you learn?

When God made Adam and Eve, He told them to have many children and fill the earth. And they did.

After the flood, Noah's three sons began having children and grandchildren. As the number of people on earth began to grow again, God told Noah's family to spread out and start to cover the earth. God created this big, wide world, and He wanted humans to care for all the land, not just one big city. He wanted them to help one another and to remind one another of His great promise to send His Son to save us from our sins.

But the people did not want to spread out. They wanted to stay together and build a huge city. So they found a big flat space and worked together to build a city with a huge tower. They wanted this tower to be strong and sturdy, to stretch up high into the sky.

But they weren't building this tower to remember God or to thank Him for saving them from the flood. They wanted their children and grandchildren to look at this tower and remember them forever. They wanted to be great and famous like God.

But God knew that was not good. The most important thing is for every person to remember how much God loves us and how He wants to save us from death through His Son.

God could have left them alone to do what they wanted. But He cared too much to let them all turn their backs and forget about His promises. So He decided it was better to separate them than let them stay together.

Until then, everyone had been speaking the same language. God came down and changed their one language into many different languages. Suddenly, it was as if some people were speaking English, others Chinese, others Swahili, and others Spanish. They could not understand one another. Since they couldn't understand one another, they couldn't work together. They also stopped trusting one another. So they found the people who spoke their same language and went off together to fill the earth.

That was the best thing for people, so they wouldn't keep leading one another away from God. But sadly, it makes it very hard to share God's promises with people who don't speak our same language.

Today, people speak about seven thousand different languages around the world. And many of these people do not have the Bible in their language, so they don't know about Jesus. But God's people are working hard to learn those languages so they can share the story of God's promises and of His Son, Jesus Christ, who lived and died and rose again that we might live with Him forever. Maybe you can learn a new language and share Jesus' story with people who speak that language.

LET'S PRAY: Heavenly Father, You were right to change the languages, even though that makes it hard to tell everyone about Jesus. Be with all Your people who are working hard to learn other languages so they can tell many more people about Your love and all Jesus did for us. We pray in Jesus' name. Amen.

God Calls Abram

What is the biggest promise anyone has ever given you? Did they keep that promise?

Noah's family spread out across the earth after God changed their languages at the tower of Babel. Even though they spoke different languages, they shared the same family stories in their new languages—the creation, the story of Noah and the flood, and the tower of Babel.

But the more time went by, the more people forgot how the stories went, and they started changing them. Even worse, in time, many of Noah's descendants forgot about the God who created them, loved them, and promised to send His Son to save them. Some started treating their kings and leaders like they were gods. Others treated powerful animals like gods. Still others worshiped the sun, moon, and stars as gods.

How would God keep His promise alive? Just like He chose Noah before, now He chose a man named Abram, who came from the line of Noah's son Shem. Abram was married to a woman named Sarai. Suddenly, unexpectedly, God came and called Abram by name. He told him to get up and leave his home and travel to a land God would show him.

God made three great promises to Abram. The Lord's first promise was to make Abram's family into a great nation. By itself, that was a promise that seemed too good to be true. Abram was already seventy-five years old, and Sarai was sixty-five. They didn't have a child, and everyone thought she was too old to have a baby. But Abram believed God could do anything He wanted to do, no matter what people thought.

God's second promise was to make Abram's name great. That meant people all over would know Abram, they would remember him long after he died, and they would thank God for his faith.

God's third promise was the most important of all. He would bless all the families of the earth through Abram's offspring. This was the same promise God gave Adam and Eve back in the Garden of Eden. God was now including Abram in the line that would lead to Jesus, the Son of God and Savior of the world.

Abram believed God. He got up, packed his things, and took his wife, Sarai, and Lot his nephew. He didn't know where he was going, just that God would guide him. God led them to a land called Canaan (KAY-nuhn). Abram would never build a house there; he would live in a big tent and move it from place to place in the land. We call Canaan the Promised Land because God promised He would give that land to Abram's descendants afterward.

God has made many wonderful promises to you. He promised to save you through Jesus and to take care of you all through life. God always keeps His promises, no matter how hard they seem.

LET'S PRAY: Heavenly Father, thank You for calling Abram to follow You. Thank You also for keeping Your promise to send one of his descendants to be the Savior, Your Son, Jesus Christ. Amen.

Abram's Visitors from Heaven

Describe a time you prayed but God didn't seem to do anything.

Twenty-four years had passed since God first appeared to Abram. Abram was living in a tent in the Promised Land, still waiting for God to give him the son He promised. Suddenly, God appeared and promised Abram he would become the father of many nations. God changed Abram's name to Abraham. He changed Sarai's name to Sarah. He commanded Abraham to be circumcised along with every boy and man in his family. Every new baby boy had to be circumcised when he was eight days old. This would remind Abraham and the great nation God would raise up from him that they were God's special people.

Later that same year, Abraham was sitting in the shady doorway of his tent in the hottest part of the day. He looked up to see three men standing in front of him. He jumped to his feet and asked them to stay so could give them some food.

He did not know that two of the men were angels and the third was God Himself. While He was eating, God gave Abraham a thrilling promise, "I will surely return to you about this time next year, and Sarah your wife shall have a son."

Sarah was sitting inside the tent, listening to the Stranger. When she thought about having a baby at age 89, she couldn't keep from laughing.

God asked Abraham, "Why did Sarah laugh? Is anything too hard for the Lord? I will return to you, about this time next year, and Sarah shall have a son." Sarah was afraid. From inside the tent, she said, "I did not laugh." But God knew better. He said, "No, but you did laugh."

One year later, He gave her the child He promised. When the baby was born, they named him Isaac (EYE-zuhk), which means "he laughs." Sarah said, "God has made laughter for me; everyone who hears will laugh over me." God kept His promise, and Sarah was so happy she couldn't stop laughing.

Abraham and Sarah had to wait twenty-five years, but more than two thousand years had already gone by since God first promised to send His own Son, Jesus. Another two thousand years after Isaac was born to Sarah, Jesus was born to Mary. When Mary laid God's Son down in a manger that first Christmas in Bethlehem, angels sang and shepherds and Wise Men laughed in joy.

Sometimes we pray to God and ask Him for something. We wait and wait, and nothing seems to happen. It seems like God does not hear us or that He does not care. But God always hears our prayers, and He cares about us so much He sent Jesus to suffer and die for us. So when we pray, it would be a good idea to ask God to give us wisdom to learn His answer and patience to wait for it.

LET'S PRAY: God our Father, thank You for keeping Your promises, especially Your promise to send Your Son into our world to save us. Fill our hearts with laughter always, so we will gladly tell others what You have done for us. In Jesus' name. Amen.

God Rescues Lot

What is the scariest place you've ever been?

Abraham made dinner for God and the two angels. After dinner, God sent the two angels to a city called Sodom (SOD-uhm). The Lord stayed and told Abraham He was going to destroy the city because the people were so bad. Abraham then thought of his nephew Lot.

Lot was the son of Abraham's brother Haran (HER-uhn). After Haran died, Lot went to live with Abraham and Sarah and went with them to the Promised Land. But God gave them so many cattle and sheep there wasn't enough grass to feed them all. So Lot moved away to live in Sodom.

Abraham knew Lot had a wife and two daughters. That made four believers. He asked God to save Sodom if He found ten believers in it. God said He would. If they could find a few more believers, Sodom could be saved.

That evening, Lot sat in the city gate. He saw two strangers walking toward him. They were the two angels who had come from Abraham and God.

Lot did not know they were angels. He was worried they would not be safe, so he asked them to come and stay in his house for the night. They told him they would happily sleep out on the street, but Lot didn't give up, so they went in with him.

Late at night, the men of Sodom gathered around Lot's house and banged on his door. They told Lot to bring out the two strangers so they could attack them.

Lot begged them to leave the men alone, but the people told him they would break down his door and treat him worse than the two strangers. Suddenly, the angels reached out and pulled Lot back inside the house and shut the door. They struck the men of Sodom blind so they could not see.

Then they asked Lot if he had anyone else living in the city. Lot talked to two men who were going to marry his daughters, hoping they would believe in God too. He warned them that God was about to destroy Sodom. But the men didn't believe God's warning and refused to leave.

The angels told Lot he and his family must run to the mountains right away. They led him out of the city, along with his wife and daughters. They told them, "Don't look back!"

Behind them, Lot and his family heard the roar of fire coming down from heaven onto Sodom. Lot's wife turned around to look, and God changed her to a pillar of salt. Lot and his daughters were very, very scared, but they keep running and safely escaped the fires.

God saved Lot from the fiery destruction of Sodom, just as He had saved Noah from the flood. He warns us that on the Last Day He will destroy this world with fire. But He promises to save everyone who believes in Jesus. We don't need to be afraid. But we should tell our family and friends so they can put their trust in Jesus and be safe.

LET'S PRAY: Lord God, Judgment Day will be very scary for the people who don't believe in Jesus. Thank You for giving me faith. Help me tell others as Lot did. In Jesus' name. Amen.

God Tests Abraham

What is the hardest thing anyone has ever asked you to do?

Abraham loved his son Isaac very much. He knew Isaac's children would grow into a great nation—and even better, many years later, one of Isaac's children would be God's promised Son, our Savior.

So Abraham must have been surprised and confused the day God told him, "Take your son, your only son Isaac, whom you love, and go to the land of Moriah (moh-RYE-uh), and offer him there as a burnt offering on one of the mountains of which I shall tell you."

Why would God want Abraham to kill his own son? This was the child God had promised! This was the child through whom God's own Son would come! Abraham didn't understand, but he loved God and did what the Lord told him to do. He got up early the next morning, cut the wood for the offering, put a saddle on his donkey, and started out with Isaac and two servants.

Three days later, Abraham saw the mountain in the distance. He told his servants, "Stay here with the donkey; I and the boy will go over there and worship and come again to you." He laid the wood on Isaac, while he carried the fire and the knife to kill his son.

As they climbed the mountain together, Isaac turned to his father and asked, "My father!" Abraham answered, "Here I am, my son." Isaac said, "Behold, the fire and the wood, but where is the lamb for a burnt offering?" Abraham told him, "God will provide for Himself the lamb for a burnt offering, my son."

At the top of the mountain, Abraham stacked up the wood, tied up Isaac, and laid him on the wood. Then Abraham took the knife and raised it above his son, ready to sacrifice him.

But the angel of the Lord called out to him, "Abraham, Abraham!" He answered, "Here I am." The angel said, "Do not lay your hand on the boy or do anything to him, for now I know that you fear God, seeing you have not withheld your son, your only son, from Me."

Abraham looked around and saw a ram caught in a thorny bush by its horns. Abraham untied Isaac and offered the ram in place of Isaac.

God never wanted Abraham to kill Isaac. He wanted to test Abraham to see if he trusted God's promises or if he loved his son more than God. But God did something more. He showed us a little more clearly what would happen to Jesus, the Savior He had promised to Adam and Eve in the garden.

Like Abraham, God the Father took His only Son, Jesus—the one He loves—and sacrificed Him for us. Just like Isaac carried the wood for the sacrifice, Jesus carried the wooden cross to Mount Calvary, very close to Mount Moriah. Jesus is the Lamb of God, who died for you and me.

LET'S PRAY: Heavenly Father, thank You for helping us understand that You loved us so much You gave up Your only Son, Jesus, to save us. And Jesus, thank You for carrying Your cross to this mountain to die for all of us. Amen.

Isaac and Rebekah

Describe something you asked God to do for you.

Abraham offered the ram on Mount Moriah and then took Isaac back home. Isaac grew up and kept sheep and cows like his father. When Isaac was 37 and Abraham was 137, Sarah died.

Abraham and Isaac were very sad, but Abraham knew it was time to find a wife for Isaac. Many young women lived nearby, but they did not believe in God. So Abraham told his servant to go back to his homeland and bring back a young woman from his family to become Isaac's wife.

The servant was afraid this would be hard. How would he find a woman who would leave her family, move far away, and marry a man she had never met? Abraham promised him God would go with him and give him success.

The servant went to the town of Abraham's family and stood by a spring of water. The young women were coming out to draw water. He asked God to show him which of these girls He had chosen for Isaac. He told the Lord he would ask the girls for a drink of water. Then he asked God to have the right girl give him water and water his camels too.

Before he finished praying, a young woman walked up to the spring of water. He asked her for a drink, and she gave him water. After he drank, she poured water for his camels too. Abraham's servant could see she was kind and good. He gave her a gold ring and two bracelets from Abraham. Then he asked her father's name, and if he had enough room for him to stay at his house that night. She told him her name was Rebekah. Her father was Bethuel (BETH-oo-el), and her grandfather was Nahor (nuh-HOR). The servant smiled because Nahor was Abraham's brother. God had answered his prayer.

Rebekah ran home and told her family about this stranger. Her brother Laban (LAY-buhn) rushed out to bring Abraham's servant to their house. The servant told them how God had blessed Abraham, had given him many sheep and cattle, and had given him a son by Sarah in his old age.

Then he told how Abraham had sent him to find a wife for Isaac. He told about his prayer at the spring and how Rebekah gave water to him and his camels. Then he asked her father, Bethuel, if he would let her go with him and become Isaac's wife.

Bethuel said yes, but he wanted to ask Rebekah. Rebekah said yes, she would go. Early the next morning, she left with the servant to go marry Isaac. God would keep Jesus' line going through Isaac and Rebekah's son.

It is always good for us to pray and ask God to guide us wherever we are and whatever we are doing. We can be sure He will answer our prayers, guide our paths through life, and set before us opportunities to serve Him and other people day by day.

LET'S PRAY: Lord God, thank You for watching over us and providing everything we need. Remind me to pray to You, because You promise to answer all my prayers for Jesus' sake. Amen.

Jacob and Esau

Is there something you really want God to do for you?

Isaac and Rebekah were married, but no baby came. Isaac prayed to God, and after twenty years He gave them twins. God told Rebekah the younger twin would be greater than the older.

The oldest twin was hairy and red, so Isaac and Rebekah called him Esau (EE-saw), which means "hairy," and also Edom, which means "red." While he was being born, they noticed the younger twin holding onto Esau's heel. They called him Jacob, which means "someone who cheats."

Esau grew up to be a good hunter. Isaac loved him best because his food tasted so good. But Rebekah loved Jacob best because he spent time with her in the house, and she remembered God's promise about Jacob.

But neither brother really thought about God at all. One day, Esau came home from the field very hungry. He wanted some red stew Jacob was eating. Jacob should have shared, but instead he said he would trade it for Esau's birthright. Esau said, "I am about to die; of what use is a birthright to me?"

But the birthright was very important. It decided which son would lead the family after the father died, and for Jacob and Esau, it showed which son would be in God's promised line. Esau didn't really care about that, so he sold his right to be in Jesus' line for a bowl of stew.

Many years later, Isaac was so old he couldn't see anymore. He wanted to give Esau God's great blessing before he died. He told Esau to go hunt and bring him a wonderful meal so he could bless him. This was very important to Esau because he wanted to be wealthy like his father.

Rebekah overheard and decided to trick Isaac so he would give Jacob the blessing God promised. While Esau hunted, she cooked Isaac a delicious meal. She had Jacob wear Esau's clothes so he would smell like him. Then she put goat skins on Jacob's hands and neck so Isaac would feel them and think it was hairy Esau instead of smooth-skinned Jacob.

And Rebekah's plan worked. Isaac thought Jacob was Esau. He ate Jacob's food and then gave him many blessings to make him great and help build his family. Right after Jacob left, Esau brought his delicious food to Isaac. Isaac realized he had been tricked, but he had little to give Esau because Jacob already had his blessing.

Esau was so angry that he planned to kill Jacob. Rebekah learned about his plan and asked Isaac to send Jacob back to her family to find a wife. She knew he would be safe there. Isaac sent Jacob on his way.

Rebekah and Jacob did a very bad thing when they tricked Isaac. They should have trusted God to give Jacob the blessings He had promised. But Isaac did a bad thing too. Instead of listening to God, he tried to give his blessing to his favorite child, not God's choice. Sometimes we want to do things our own way. But God's way is always best.

LET'S PRAY: Heavenly Father, thank You for keeping the line of people that led to Your Son, Jesus. Give us faith to live for You and strength to forgive the people who sin against us. We pray in Jesus' name. Amen.

Jacob's Dream

Describe a time you felt scared and all alone.

Esau was furious at Jacob for tricking their father and taking his blessings. He did not want to upset Isaac, so he decided to wait until his father died. Then he would kill Jacob. Rebekah learned about Esau's plan and told Isaac it was time to get a wife for Jacob. She did not want him to marry the women who lived around them because they did not believe in the true God. She asked Isaac to send him to her brother Laban to get a wife. Isaac agreed and sent Jacob far away.

Jacob was nervous. He had never traveled this way before, and he had to live with his uncle Laban, a man he had never met. One evening, he stopped to sleep for the night. He took a rock and used it for his pillow. How do you think that would feel to lay your head on a rock?

In the night, as Jacob slept, God gave him a special dream. Jacob was standing at the bottom of a huge set of steps that rose up out of the ground and reached clear up into heaven. He saw angels going up and down on the steps because God was sending them to help people.

Jacob saw God standing at the top of the steps. God told him, "The land on which you lie I will give to you and your offspring. Your offspring shall be like the dust of the earth, and in you and your offspring shall all the families of the earth be blessed."

Jacob was shocked. This same promise God had given to Abraham and Isaac. Now Jacob knew he was in the family line that would give us the Savior God promised long ago.

Before this dream, Jacob hadn't really thought about God very much. If he had, he wouldn't have tricked his father and his brother. But after the dream, he knew God was watching over him.

When he woke up, he stood up the rock that was his pillow and poured oil on it to set it aside as something special. He said, "Surely the Lord is in this place, and I did not know it." He was afraid and said, "How awesome is this place! This is none other than the house of God, and this is the gate of heaven."

He made a promise to God, "If God will be with me and will keep me in this way that I go, and will give me bread to eat and clothing to wear, so that I come again to my father's house in peace, then the Lord shall be my God, and this stone, which I have set up for a pillar, shall be God's house."

All through our lives, Jesus is with us, no matter where we are, no matter what we are doing. We may feel scared and alone, but we are never really alone. Jesus is always here to guard us, give us what we need, and answer our prayers.

LET'S PRAY: Lord God, thank You for watching over Jacob and giving him Your promise. Remind me that You will always go with me and protect me, and You will bless me for Jesus' sake. Amen.

35

Jacob's Family

Describe a time you tried to be nice to someone but that person treated you badly.

Jacob traveled to the land where Abraham lived before he came to the Promised Land. He was looking for a wife from the daughters of his uncle Laban.

At the well outside of town, Jacob met Laban's younger daughter, Rachel. He rolled away a huge stone and watered her sheep. When Rachel learned he was her aunt Rebekah's son, she ran to tell her father. Laban ran to Jacob, hugged him, and brought him to his house.

Jacob stayed a month, taking care of Laban's sheep. During that month, he fell in love with Rachel. Laban told Jacob he wanted to pay him for all his hard work and agreed to let him marry Rachel if he would stay and work seven more years. Jacob was delighted.

Before Jacob had come, Laban did not have many sheep. But during these seven years, God blessed everything Jacob did. Laban's flocks grew really large.

When the wedding day came, Laban held a great feast and invited many guests. But he was afraid Jacob would move away and his flocks would stop growing. So he waited until night, and then when Jacob couldn't see, he switched his older daughter Leah for Rachel.

When the sun came up the next morning, Jacob saw that Laban tricked him. He complained, but Laban told him that in his country the older sisters got married first. Laban promised to let Jacob marry Rachel, too, if he would be his shepherd for seven more years. One week later, Jacob married Rachel too.

Jacob loved Rachel but hated Leah. The two sisters were jealous of each other and fought a lot. Between Leah and Rachel and their two servant girls, God gave Jacob twelve sons and a daughter named Dinah.

Jacob finished the seven years he promised Laban for Rachel. Then he wanted to leave with his family, but Laban did not want to lose God's blessings. He asked Jacob to stay. Jacob said he would stay if he could have all the speckled and spotted sheep and black lambs. But before Jacob came for the sheep, Laban separated those sheep out and sent them far away with his sons. Jacob came and found no spotted or speckled sheep and no black lambs. But he kept his promise and took care of Laban's sheep.

God protected Jacob and made sure his flocks grew and Laban's got smaller. Laban kept changing which sheep would be Jacob's, but God always gave Jacob the strong lambs and Laban the weaker ones. Slowly, Jacob's flocks grew larger and larger, while Laban's shrunk smaller and smaller.

God always watches over you, just like He watched over Jacob. When people cheat against us, that makes God unhappy. But God watches over us and always takes care of us. He helps us tell the truth, keep our promises, and do good to other people. We pray they will see God's love in us.

LET'S PRAY: Heavenly Father, thank You for watching over Jacob, even when his uncle Laban tricked him. Since You promise to watch over me, help me be honest and treat everyone well, so they can see Your love in me and trust in Jesus too. In Jesus' name. Amen.

Jacob Returns Home

Describe a time someone made you really mad. What did it feel like the next time you saw that person?

It had been twenty years since Jacob had first come to Laban, and in that time God had given him two wives, eleven of his twelve sons, a daughter named Dinah, and other daughters too. He had large herds and flocks, camels and donkeys, and many servants.

But Jacob wanted to go back home because Laban was not being nice to him anymore. Laban thought all the animals and servants should be his. But God took them away and gave them to Jacob because Laban was not honest and fair. The Lord told Jacob, "Return to the land of your fathers and to your kindred, and I will be with you."

Jacob gathered his family, his animals, and his things together and sneaked away from Laban without telling him. Three days later, Laban found out and chased after him. But the night before they met, God warned Laban not to say anything to Jacob. Jacob promised Laban he would treat his daughters well, and they agreed they would not harm each other.

After that, Jacob thought about meeting his brother, Esau, again. But he was very, very scared. Twenty years ago, Esau had wanted to kill him after he stole Isaac's blessing. So Jacob sent servants to tell Esau he was coming home. His servants came back and told him Esau was coming down to meet him with four hundred men. Jacob was terribly afraid. He thought Esau was bringing these men to attack and kill his family.

That night, he picked some of his animals as presents to give to Esau. He hoped the gifts would turn away Esau's anger. Then he sent his family across a brook of water and stayed behind to pray.

While he was praying, a stranger came and started wrestling with him. They wrestled through the night. When the sun rose, the stranger told him he had to leave, but Jacob wouldn't let go. The stranger touched Jacob's hip and hurt it very badly, but Jacob held on tight. Through his pain and tears, he said, "I will not let You go unless You bless me." He learned this stranger was God Himself, and he bowed down before Him. God gave him a new name, Israel (IZ-ray-uhl). The name means "he wrestles." Israel would be the name of the great nation God would raise out of Jacob's twelve sons.

Israel got up, limped across the brook, and went to meet Esau. Esau saw him, ran up, and wrapped his arms around him. Over these twenty years, God had helped Esau forgive his brother. He brought the four hundred men only to protect Israel and his family until they got safely home.

Sometimes we do bad things to people. They get really mad at us, and we are afraid to see them again . . . afraid of what they will say or do. God taught Israel to pray and never give up. Like him, you can pray to God too.

LET'S PRAY: Lord God, thank You for preparing Esau's heart to forgive Israel and receive him back happily. Forgive me where I do wrong, and help the people I hurt learn to love and forgive me too. And help me forgive the people who hurt me. In Jesus' name. Amen.

Joseph's Dreams

Who is your favorite friend? What makes that person your favorite?

When Israel came back to the Promised Land, he brought his eleven sons. One day, they were traveling close to Bethlehem and Rachel started giving birth to a second baby. She had a lot of trouble and died after her son was born. Israel was very sad to lose the wife he loved the most. He named her baby Benjamin, which means "son of the right hand." He was the last of Israel's twelve sons.

But of all his twelve sons, Israel loved one far more than the others. This son was Joseph, Rachel's firstborn. Israel gave him a very special, beautiful robe much, much nicer than any clothes his brothers had. That made Joseph's brothers jealous and angry.

It got worse when Joseph saw four of his brothers doing something bad and then rushed home to tell Israel and get them in trouble. They were so mad they couldn't even say a kind word to him.

But it got even worse. God gave Joseph two special dreams. In the first dream, Joseph and his brothers were cutting down plants in a field and tying them together. In his dream, his plants stood up tall, while his brothers' plants all bowed down before his. When he told his brothers this dream, they got mad because they were older—they said they would never bow down to him.

Then Joseph had a second dream. In it, the sun, the moon, and eleven stars were bowing down to him. When he told his brothers this dream, they realized they were the eleven stars, their father, Israel, was the sun, and their mother was the moon. They were so furious they could not talk with him. They couldn't even stand to be in the same room with him. Even Israel thought Joseph had gone too far this time. He thought children should respect their parents. He told Joseph he shouldn't talk that way about his dream. But Israel made sure to remember that dream.

In the future, those dreams would be very important to Joseph. He would soon go through some really, really hard times. And these dreams would remind him that he was still in God's plans—even when it didn't feel like it.

Having a favorite friend is not a bad thing—it's a really good thing when God gives you a close friend. It's a good thing as long as you treat all your other friends well. That was Israel's problem—he let all of his children know he loved Joseph the most. It is no wonder Joseph wanted to boast and show off.

It was hard to be Joseph's brothers, knowing their father loved him more than them. But Joseph's brothers should not have hated him the way they did. Only God could take away their anger and help them love him like they should.

LET'S PRAY: Heavenly Father, thank You for loving me and making me Your very own child. Help me not to think I am better than all other children but to remember You love each of us, so I can be kind and good to all my brothers and sisters in Jesus. Amen.

Joseph's Troubles

Have you ever gotten in trouble for something you didn't do?

Joseph's brothers were so jealous they couldn't stand to listen to him talk. Like Cain and Esau, they held their anger inside—and bad things happen when we hold our anger inside.

Joseph's brothers were out watching the sheep. Israel sent Joseph to check on them. The brothers saw Joseph coming to them wearing that special robe, and it made them really angry. They wanted to kill him so his dreams would not come true. But Israel's oldest son, Reuben, cared about his father. He knew Israel's heart would break if Joseph was killed. So he convinced his brothers to put Joseph into a pit instead. After they left, he planned to come back and pull Joseph out again.

But while Reuben was gone, the fourth brother, Judah, said, "Let's not kill him; he is our brother, after all. Let's sell him as a slave instead." The brothers liked that idea, so they pulled him out of the pit, took his robe away from him, and sold him to some men who were traveling down to Egypt.

Reuben came back and saw the pit was empty. He was so upset at his brothers that he tore his clothes and then asked what he was going to say when their father asked where Joseph was. The brothers took a goat and killed it. They took Joseph's fancy robe, tore it, and dipped it in the goat's blood. They would trick their father, Israel, into thinking a wild animal attacked and killed Joseph.

When Israel saw the coat, he believed the brothers' lie. He was so sad and upset that no one could make him happy again, no matter how hard they tried.

Joseph was taken to Egypt and sold as a slave to a man named Potiphar (POT-ih-fuhr).

God was with Joseph and helped him do everything well. In time, Potiphar trusted Joseph and liked him so much that he put him in charge of everything in his house.

But Potiphar's wife thought Joseph was very handsome. She wanted him to fall in love with her—but Joseph knew better than that. She was Potiphar's wife. He would not sin against Potiphar, and he would not sin against God. That made Potiphar's wife very mad. She lied to her husband, telling him Joseph was trying to hurt her. Potiphar got so mad he threw Joseph into a terrible prison.

But just like at Potiphar's house, God was with Joseph. He did such a good job, the jailer asked him to take care of all the other prisoners.

Joseph's brothers did something terrible to him, and when he was in Egypt there was nothing he could do but be kind and friendly, work as hard as he could, and trust God to take care of him. When someone does something bad to you, God will take care of you, and He will help you be strong like Joseph.

LET'S PRAY: God our Father, thank You for being with Joseph when his brothers treated him badly and he was thrown into prison. Help me when my life gets hard because other people treat me badly. In Jesus' name. Amen.

Joseph Feeds Egypt

Describe a time you did something really nice for someone and the person didn't thank you.

Joseph worked hard for Potiphar, but he threw Joseph in prison when his wife lied and told him Joseph tried to hurt her. But God made the jailer like Joseph so much that he put him in charge of all the other prisoners.

Later, Pharaoh (FAIR-oh), the king of Egypt, got mad at two men and sent them to prison. One was the cupbearer who brought him drinks, and the other was the chief baker.

One morning, they were both upset because they had dreams they couldn't understand. Joseph asked them to tell him their dreams, and God would tell him what they meant.

The cupbearer dreamed of a vine with three branches that flowered and grew grapes. He squeezed them into wine and brought the wine to Pharaoh. Joseph told him that in three days the king would take him out of prison and make him cupbearer again. He asked the cupbearer to remember him.

Then the chief baker told his dream. He was carrying three baskets of food to Pharaoh. But birds were eating it out of the basket on his head. Joseph told him that in three days Pharaoh would take him out of prison and kill him.

Three days later, Pharaoh had a birthday party. He released the cupbearer, but he killed the baker. The cupbearer was so happy that he forgot all about Joseph. Two whole years went by, and Joseph was still in prison.

Then one day, Pharaoh had a dream that made him worry. Seven strong, fat cows came up out of the Nile River and fed along the shore. Then seven thin, ugly cows came up and ate the fat ones. But they stayed just as skinny. Pharaoh woke up.

When he fell back asleep again, he had a second dream. In this dream, he saw a plant with seven good, healthy ears of grain. Then seven ugly, empty ears sprouted. While he watched, the bad ears ate up the seven good ears.

None of Pharaoh's wise men could tell him what these dreams meant. But the cupbearer remembered how God told Joseph all about his dream and the chief baker's dream. So Joseph was cleaned up and brought to Pharaoh.

Joseph told Pharaoh the seven good cows and seven good ears of grain meant there would be seven good years with a whole lot of food growing in the fields. But then seven terrible years would come when no food would grow. He told Pharaoh to gather extra food during the seven good years so there would be food to eat when the seven bad years came.

Pharaoh freed Joseph from prison and put him in charge of everything in Egypt. Joseph stored up lots of food before the seven bad years came.

God was with Joseph during those hard years in prison. God promises to be with you always, whether your life is good or bad. And like Joseph, you will find that God will make everything work out for your good.

LET'S PRAY: Lord God, thank You for helping Joseph all through those hard years in prison and bringing him to Egypt to save so many people. Remind me You will always take care of me. I pray in Jesus' name. Amen.

Joseph Forgives His Brothers Genesis 42–45

How hard is it to love someone who has done something bad to you?

Food wouldn't grow in Egypt. It wouldn't grow in the Promised Land either. When Jacob learned Egypt was selling food, he sent his ten oldest sons to buy some.

When they got to Egypt, Joseph knew who they were right away, but they didn't know it was Joseph. If he wanted, he could have been really mean—just like they had been to him. But God had helped him forgive them. Before he revealed himself, Joseph would be God's instrument to drive his brothers to repentance. He said they were bad men who did not come for food but to learn the secrets of Egypt. He put all of them in prison.

After three days, Joseph freed each of them except Simeon. He told them they could buy food this time, but they had to bring back their youngest brother or Simeon wouldn't get out of jail, and they wouldn't be able to buy more food.

The brothers rushed home and told their father, Israel, what happened. They wanted to go right back with Benjamin, but Israel wouldn't let him go. He couldn't lose Benjamin like he had lost Joseph and Simeon.

After they ate up all the food, Israel told them to go back and buy more. His son Judah told him they had to bring Benjamin back. Finally, Israel agreed and sent Benjamin. Joseph brought Simeon out of prison and gave them a big feast.

Then came the real test. Joseph's servants filled the brothers' bags with food and then put Joseph's special silver cup in Benjamin's bag. When the brothers started home, the servant stopped them and asked who stole the cup. When they opened their bags, the cup was in Benjamin's bag.

They all cried and went back to Joseph. He told them Benjamin had to go to jail, but they were free to go back home because they were honest. But Judah begged Joseph to let him go to prison in Benjamin's place. He couldn't go home to his father without Benjamin.

Finally, Joseph knew his brothers were really sorry for what they did to him. He told them, "I am Joseph! Is my father still alive?"

He told them to rush home and bring Jacob to come and live with him in Egypt. When Israel learned Joseph was alive and ruling in Egypt, he praised God. He said, "Joseph my son is still alive. I will go and see him before I die." So Israel took his whole family and all his animals, and they went to live with Joseph in Egypt.

This true story ends the Book of Genesis, the book of beginnings. We read about the beginning of the world, people, and sin. We read about the beginning of God's promises to send His Son, and His promises to Abraham, Isaac, and Israel. Next, in the Book of Exodus, we will see Israel grow into a great nation.

LET'S PRAY: Heavenly Father, thank You for helping Joseph forgive his brothers and bringing Israel to be with him again. Give me the love I need to forgive those who sin against me, just as You forgive my sins for Jesus' sake. Amen.

Birth of Moses

Describe how it feels to be bullied.

At the end of Genesis, Israel (Jacob) moved his family to Egypt, where Joseph could take care of them. When Jacob died, Joseph and his brothers took Jacob's body back to the Promised Land and buried him with his parents. The twelve brothers went back to Egypt and lived there until they died. Their children and grandchildren stayed in Egypt, growing into the nation God had promised Abraham long before.

Many years later, a new pharaoh became king in Egypt. He didn't remember how Joseph, an Israelite, saved Egypt during the seven bad years. He just knew Israel had grown big and strong, and he was afraid of them. He decided to make sure they wouldn't be stronger than he was by making them his slaves. He had his people be mean to the Israelites and make them do hard and dirty work. It made the Israelites very sad to be bullied and treated so badly.

God saw how badly the Egyptians were treating His people, the Israelites. God loved the Israelites and blessed them. They became a very great nation and became very strong from all the hard work they were forced to do. Pharaoh became so scared of the Israelites that he decided to do something really bad. He commanded that every Israelite baby boy should be thrown into the Nile River.

God wanted His people, the Israelites, to live and stay strong. An Israelite woman who trusted God and wasn't afraid of Pharaoh's law had a baby boy and hid him until he was too old to keep hidden any longer. She made a basket that would float in the river out of plants that grow along the shore and tar. She put her baby in the basket and placed it in the river among the plants and told her daughter Miriam to follow along the bank to watch and see what would happen to him.

That same morning, Pharaoh's daughter came out to wash herself in the river. She saw the basket floating among the river plants. When her servant brought her the basket, she looked inside and saw a crying baby. She knew it was a little Israelite boy. Her father would have wanted her to pull out that baby and throw him into the river. But she felt sorry for him. She took him from the basket and carried him into Pharaoh's house as her own son. She named him Moses, which means "draw out," because she pulled him out of the water.

God sometimes does funny things to people who try to go against Him. Pharaoh was feeding, clothing, teaching, and raising the very Israelite boy God had chosen to lead Israel out of Egypt when he grew up.

The same thing later happened to Jesus when He was little. A king ordered his soldiers to kill every baby boy. But God kept Jesus safe by having Joseph take Mary and Jesus to Egypt to hide there.

There are times when it is not easy to be God's child. But God is always with us. He sends angels to protect us, and He gives us all we need to stay strong in faith and joyful even when life is hard and sad.

LET'S PRAY: Lord God, Pharaoh tried very hard to hurt Your people and destroy the baby You chose to set Your people free. Thank You for protecting Moses. Thank You also for protecting Jesus when He was a little child and another king tried to kill Him. Remind me You will always protect me too. For Jesus' sake. Amen.

Moses and the Burning Bush

Exodus 2:11–4:17

Describe a time you saw someone who needed your help. What did you do?

Moses grew up in Pharaoh's house. He was raised and taught as a prince of Egypt. But Moses knew he was really an Israelite. When he was forty years old, Moses had a tough choice to make. Should he live as an Egyptian prince so he could help the Israelites in secret? Or should he tell people he was really an Israelite?

One day, he went out to look at the Israelites and got upset when he saw an Egyptian beating an Israelite slave. Moses decided to help the slave. He looked around to make sure no one was watching, and then he attacked the Egyptian and killed him.

The next day, Moses saw one Israelite slave beating up another. Moses stepped between them and asked, "Why are you hitting your friend?" The slave answered, "Who made you a prince and a judge over us? Do you plan to kill me as you killed the Egyptian?" Moses was scared that people knew he had killed the Egyptian. He was afraid Pharaoh would find out, so he quickly left Egypt and went out in the desert to a land called Midian.

In Midian, he met seven sisters watering their sheep at a well. They worked hard to pull up all that water, but some other shepherds came and stole it. Moses stepped in and made them wait their turn while the girls went first. The girls' father invited Moses to stay with them, and Moses married his daughter Zipporah (zih-POH-ruh).

For forty years, Moses lived in Midian, being a shepherd for his wife's father. Then one day, he saw something strange on a nearby mountain called Mount Horeb (HOH-reb) (also known as Mount Sinai [SIGH-nigh]). A bush was on fire, but it didn't burn up. So he went over to learn how this was happening.

When he got close, he heard a voice. It called out, "Moses! Moses! Do not come near; take your sandals off your feet, for the place on which you are standing is holy ground." God was in the fire. He told Moses He had seen how badly the Egyptians were treating the Israelite slaves. He told Moses to go back to Egypt to set the Israelites free.

Three times, Moses had seen people being bullied and had stepped in to help them. But this time, he wasn't so quick to go. He was eighty years old, and it had been forty years since he left Egypt. He was afraid Pharaoh wouldn't listen to him and the Israelites wouldn't believe God sent him. He also had trouble talking very well.

God sent Moses' brother Aaron to do the talking for Moses. The Lord promised He would go with Moses and work great and powerful miracles to force Pharaoh to set the Israelites free.

Like Moses, you can keep watching for people at school or in your neighborhood who need your help. Remember that God sent Jesus to rescue you from the devil.

LET'S PRAY: Lord God, You sent Moses to lead Your people out of slavery in Egypt. Thank You for also sending Your Son, Jesus, to lead us out of hell. In Jesus' name. Amen.

Moses and the Plagues

Talk about a time you really thought you were right about something but later found out you were wrong.

In the burning bush on Mount Horeb, God told Moses to go to Pharaoh with his brother Aaron and free Israel. But Pharaoh was proud and powerful. He would not set Israel free just because their God told him to. Moses warned him God would send plagues (PLAYGZ) that would harm Egypt. Pharaoh didn't care. He would not listen to God or to Moses.

In the first plague, God turned the water in the Nile River to blood. Many fish died and no one could use the water. But Pharaoh's magicians could turn water into blood too, so he thought Moses was just doing a magic trick. Pharaoh hardened his heart—that means he refused to do what God told him to do.

The second plague brought many frogs up out of the Nile River. The frogs were everywhere—even in Pharaoh's bed! Pharaoh's magicians could make frogs come too—but they couldn't make them go. So Pharaoh asked Moses to pray for God to take the frogs away, and God made them die. But with the frogs dead, Pharaoh hardened his heart again.

The third plague brought clouds of gnats, tiny flying bugs that bit. Pharaoh's magicians tried, but they couldn't do this with their tricks. They told Pharaoh Moses wasn't doing tricks—this was really God. But Pharaoh wouldn't listen to them. He wouldn't set Israel free.

The fourth plague brought many, many flies. They got in the Egyptians' houses and were a real bother.

The fifth plague killed the Egyptians' cows, sheep, horses, donkeys, and camels, but Pharaoh still refused to obey God.

The sixth plague struck the Egyptian people. Their skin was covered with boils—painful sores. Pharaoh still said no.

Moses warned Pharaoh the seventh plague would bring lightning and huge hailstones falling from the sky. Some Egyptians believed Moses. They moved their animals and workers under shelter. The hail killed any animals and people left outside, and it destroyed half of the food growing in the fields. Pharaoh told Moses he would release the Israelites if God stopped the hail. But when the hail ended, Pharaoh changed his mind and refused.

The eighth plague was huge swarms of locusts. A locust looks kind of like a grasshopper. They covered the fields and ate up all the plants that the hail left.

The ninth plague was thick darkness that came over Egypt for three days and three nights. But once again, Pharaoh refused to let the Israelites go—even though the plagues had ruined his country.

When God tells us we are doing something right, it is good to be stubborn and refuse to change—that's what Moses and Aaron did. But when we disobey God and stubbornly refuse to change our minds, like Pharaoh, that is very bad. It will really hurt us, as it really hurt Pharaoh.

LET'S PRAY: Almighty God, You are patient and kind, but You are also firm and strong. You punished Jesus on the cross so You won't have to punish me. Teach me not to be proud and stubborn like Pharaoh, but to listen and believe everything You tell me in the Bible. In Jesus' name. Amen.

The Passover

What would your mom or dad do if they found you playing with fire? What would they do if they caught you playing with it after they told you not to?

Pharaoh refused to set Israel free, even after God sent nine powerful plagues. Do you think God was having fun destroying Pharaoh and Egypt? No. If God wanted to be mean and nasty, He could have killed Pharaoh right away and set the people of Israel free. But think carefully about those nine plagues and you will learn something important about God.

The first four plagues didn't really hurt Pharaoh or his people. It is like your mom or dad seeing you holding matches or a lighter. At first, they might take away the matches, tell you they are not toys, and say you should never play with them. If you never grab the matches or lighter again, they aren't going to punish you, are they? Of course not. And if Pharaoh would have set Israel free after the first four plagues, none of the worse plagues would have happened.

God didn't hate Pharaoh; He loved him and the people of Egypt as much as He loved the Israelites. God wanted Pharaoh to believe in Him and His promise to send a Savior so He could take away Pharaoh's sins and bring him to heaven. But Pharaoh kept playing with fire. He kept disobeying God. So God made each new plague hurt more than the last. In the end, Pharaoh brought a lot of pain on Egypt.

One final plague remained, one so horrible God waited until last to use it. Since Pharaoh refused to obey God, it was time for the last plague. At midnight, God would send the angel of death. He would go throughout Egypt and kill all the firstborn people and firstborn animals too.

But God protected the people of Israel. He told them to take a lamb, kill it, and spread its blood around the door of their houses. Then they were to cook the lamb and eat it for dinner.

At midnight, when the angel of death came to their house and saw the blood all around the doorway, it would pass over the house and leave the firstborn alive. We call that lamb the Passover lamb.

When the last plague killed Pharaoh's firstborn son, he finally set Israel free.

Many years later, God gave us a Lamb of His own—His own Son, Jesus Christ. Jesus was the Passover Lamb who died on the cross so we can live. The blood that came from the thorns on His head and the nails in His hands and feet were like the blood on the top, sides, and bottom of the doorways.

When we were baptized, we were marked by Jesus' blood, just like the doorways of the Israelites. When Jesus comes back, He will send His angels to gather all people to Himself. The angels will see Jesus' blood on us and bring us to Jesus so we can live with Him forever in heaven.

LET'S PRAY: Lord God, thank You for Your mighty Son, Jesus Christ, who died to set me free from death and hell. In Jesus' name. Amen.

Crossing the Red Sea

Describe a time you were in danger and didn't know how to get out of it.

After the angel of death killed Pharaoh's oldest son, Pharaoh finally obeyed God and freed the people of Israel. Moses led them out of Egypt. God sent an angel and a huge pillar of cloud to guide them. At the end of that first day, Israel set up their camp on the shore of the Red Sea.

But Pharaoh changed his mind again. He gathered together his whole army and rode out to bring back the Israelites as slaves. When the Israelites saw the Egyptian chariots and soldiers coming, they were afraid. They couldn't run away because the Red Sea was in the way. They started complaining and saying that Moses brought them out to kill them.

Moses told them, "Fear not, stand firm, and see the salvation of the Lord, which He will work for you today. For the Egyptians whom you see today, you shall never see again. The Lord will fight for you, and you have only to be silent."

God told Moses, "Lift up your staff, and stretch out your hand over the sea and divide it, that the people of Israel may go through the sea on dry ground." Both the angel of God and the huge pillar moved from in front of Israel to stand between them and the Egyptians. All night long, the pillar gave light to the Israelites but kept the Egyptians in darkness. It also kept the Egyptians from coming toward God's people.

Moses lifted up his staff and stretched out his hands, and the waters divided in front of them. All night long, the Israelites walked through the sea on dry ground. The Egyptians had to stay where they were because the pillar blocked them.

Finally, the Egyptians charged down into the sea after the Israelites. But God made their chariot wheels clog up. The Egyptians tried to turn back because they knew God was fighting against them. But before they could get away, God told Moses to stretch out his hand again so the waters covered the Egyptians. In a short time, not a single Egyptian was left, and Israel was truly free.

Sometimes we are scared, in trouble, and don't know what to do. That is when God tells us, "Call upon Me in the day of trouble; I will deliver you, and you shall glorify Me" (Psalm 50:15). When we pray and ask God to help, He is right there for us.

Moses told the Israelites they did not have to fight against the Egyptians; they only had to stand silently and watch God fight for them.

Jesus fought for us when He died on the cross and rose to life again three days later. We can be sure He is always here to watch us, defend us, and answer our prayers.

LET'S PRAY: Lord God, thank You for protecting Your people and showing them Your mighty power over Egypt in the Red Sea. Jesus showed that same power when He died on the cross and then rose again. Whenever I am afraid, remind me of Your great power and love. In Jesus' name. Amen.

God Provides Manna and Quail

Exodus 16

Have you ever felt so hungry you thought you were going to die? Describe how that felt.

When the Egyptian army tried to follow Israel into the Red Sea, God made their chariot wheels get clogged. Then when the last Israelite was safely on the other side of the sea, Moses stretched out his hand again and the towering walls of water came crashing down on the Egyptians.

The Israelites were very happy to be free. Moses taught them a song they could sing to thank God and always remember how He had saved them. It starts like this:

> I will sing to the LORD, for He has triumphed gloriously; the horse and his rider He has thrown into the sea. (Exodus 15:1)

The Israelites were happy and excited to be free and on their way to the Promised Land. But their happiness didn't last long. After about a month, they ran out of food and got really, really hungry. There was no food for them to eat in this wilderness, just a lot of rocks and sand.

The Israelites should have remembered what God did in Egypt and at the Red Sea. They should have trusted Him to take care of them. They should have prayed to Him and then waited for Him to give them food. Instead, they grumbled and complained.

They said they should have stayed in Egypt. They talked about all the food they could eat there—but they forgot how badly the Egyptians had treated them. They said that Moses only brought them out of Egypt so they would die in the wilderness from hunger. Even though God worked so many great miracles to set them free, they still didn't trust Him to take care of them.

So God talked to Moses. Moses told the Israelites God would send them bread and meat.

Later, when the sun started going down that evening, huge flocks of birds flew right into their camp. They were called quail. The Israelites gathered them and cooked them for supper. That was the meat God promised them.

When the sun came up the next morning, dew covered the ground. When the dew dried up in the sunshine, there was a flaky thing on the ground. The people asked Moses, "What is it?" Moses told them it was the bread God had sent from heaven. They could grind it and make bread out of it. They called it manna, which is a Hebrew word that means "What is it?"

Each day they traveled in the wilderness, God would send just enough manna for the people to eat that day.

Jesus does not want us to worry about the future, but to trust that He will always give us what we need each day. That is why He taught us to pray "give us this day our daily bread" in the Lord's Prayer (Matthew 6:11). When we pray this, Jesus reminds us how God gave manna each day to the Israelites. We can be sure He won't forget to give us what we need.

LET'S PRAY: Lord God, thank You for giving me everything I need each day. Teach me to pray to You whenever I need anything and then give You thanks when You give it to me. Teach me to trust You always. In Jesus' name. Amen.

The Ten Commandments

Describe the scariest time of your life.

God gave the Israelites manna every morning except Saturday. On that day, God wanted the Israelites to rest so they could listen to His promises and remember His gifts. But manna wasn't the only gift God gave the Israelites in the wilderness. His angel and His pillar were always with them to guide the Israelites all the way to the Promised Land. But God wanted them to make one stop along the way. It was at Mount Horeb (Sinai), where Moses saw the burning bush.

The Israelites gathered around the foot of the mountain and camped there for three days. On the third day, a thick, dark cloud came and covered the mountain. It was filled with bright lightning and booming thunder. Then a loud trumpet blast came from the mountain, making the Israelites shake in fear. God was coming down to meet them and speak with them.

The trumpet got louder and louder. Moses started talking to God, and God answered him in a loud, powerful voice. The Israelites listened while God said, "I am the Lord your God, who brought you out of the land of Egypt." Then He gave them the Ten Commandments:

You shall have no other gods.

You shall not misuse the name of the Lord your God.

Remember the Sabbath day by keeping it holy.

Honor your father and your mother.

You shall not murder.

You shall not commit adultery.

You shall not steal.

You shall not give false witness against your neighbor.

You shall not covet your neighbor's house.

You shall not covet your neighbor's wife, or his manservant or maidservant, his ox or donkey, or anything that belongs to your neighbor.

The people were trembling in fear. They were afraid they would die if God kept talking to them. They begged Moses to go up on the mountain and listen to what God wanted to tell them. They promised they would do whatever Moses said.

So Moses climbed the mountain with his helper Joshua and stayed with God forty days and forty nights.

Scary things happen to us sometimes: storms, fires, getting sick. But nothing is scarier than standing in front of God. That is because we all do bad things, and God hates bad things—He has to punish them. And that is why Judgment Day is such a scary thing for a sinner.

But that is why God sent His Son, Jesus. On the cross, Jesus stood in front of God for us. God the Father punished Him for all your sins. When you stand before Him on Judgment Day, your sins will already be gone—Jesus took them all away. He will welcome you into heaven.

LET'S PRAY: Lord God, Your Commandments show how we should live our lives. But we cannot keep them the way we should. Thank You for sending Jesus to save us. In Jesus' name. Amen.

Worship in the Tabernacle

Exodus 25–27

Have you ever made a friend so mad he or she didn't want to be your friend anymore?

On the way to the Promised Land from Egypt, God led the Israelites to Mount Sinai. There, He gave them the Ten Commandments. These teach us what we have to say and do to make God happy. The trouble was none of the Israelites could keep them, and neither can we. The Commandments show us that we make God angry and we deserve to be punished.

Here on Mount Sinai, the Lord told Moses to build a special place called the tabernacle (TAB-uhr-nak-uhl) or the tent of meeting. The tabernacle was a large, fancy tent. Inside this tent in the front was a special item that kind of looked like the altar in the front of your church—only smaller. It was called the ark of the covenant. It was covered with gold and had a golden lid with two angels carved on top. God told Moses to put the two stone tablets with the Ten Commandments and a jar of manna inside the ark (see Hebrews 9:4).

A thick curtain was set up in front of the ark to keep people from looking at it. This curtain reminded them their sins had separated them from God. And they could not come to God on their own. They needed someone special to stand between God and them to take away their sins.

That person would be God's own Son. But until He came, Moses' brother Aaron and his sons would stand in His place. We call them priests. The trouble was, Aaron and his sons were sinners too, just like you and me, just like your pastor. None of them could stand before God unless God's Son took away their sins too.

So God told Moses to use sacrifices to take away the sins of the priests and the people. Animals like sheep, goats, and bulls would die in place of the priests and the people. They would be brought to the front of the tabernacle, where they would be killed and burned on a bronze altar outside the door. All of these sacrifices and offerings pointed ahead to the day when Jesus would go to the cross and die in our place.

The ark inside the tabernacle was very important. It reminded the Israelites that God had come down to live with His people. That was why the tabernacle was a tent. As the Israelites traveled to the Promised Land, the priests would take down the tent and carry it with them. They would carry the ark with two long poles. It pointed ahead to the Son of God, who came to live with us and go from place to place teaching about God's promise.

Our sins turn God against us. But that is why Jesus went to the cross. There, He took on Himself the punishment our sins deserve. He suffered and died in our place. And right when Jesus died, the thick curtain that separated us from God was torn in two. That shows us Jesus took away all of our sins, and nothing separates us from our loving Father in heaven anymore.

LET'S PRAY: Lord God, thank You for the tabernacle, which showed us a little more about the work Jesus did when He came. Thank You for forgiving me for Jesus' sake. Amen.

The Golden Calf

Have you ever done something that made your mom or dad really, really mad?

After God spoke the Ten Commandments with His thundering voice, the Israelites were very, very scared. They begged Moses to go up and talk to God, and they promised they would do whatever Moses said. But Moses had been up on Mount Sinai for forty days. None of the people of Israel had seen him.

They told Aaron to make them gods to go in front of them and lead them. They brought him their gold, and he used fire to melt it and form a golden calf for them. The Israelites said, "These are your gods, O Israel, who brought you up out of the land of Egypt!" They made sacrifices to the calf and started dancing and celebrating.

Up on the mountain, God told Moses, "Go down, for your people, whom you brought up out of the land of Egypt have turned aside quickly out of the way I commanded them."

God was ready to send down His fire and burn them all up. Moses was scared for Israel. He prayed for God to forgive them. He reminded the Lord how He promised to make a great nation out of Abraham, Isaac, and Israel. Would He break His promise by destroying the sons of Israel now?

Moses went back down the mountain. When he saw the golden calf, he burned with anger. He threw down the two tablets with the Commandments and broke them in pieces. He burned the golden calf with fire, ground it to powder, scattered it on the water, and made the Israelites drink it.

He was really mad at Aaron. He asked him, "What did this people do to you?" Aaron lied and told Moses, "They gave the gold to me, and I threw it into the fire, and out came this calf."

The next day, Moses told the people, "You have sinned a great sin. And now I will go up to the Lord; perhaps I can make atonement (uh-TONE-muhnt)." The word *atonement* means "to pay the penalty for sin." Atonement would turn away God's anger and make things right between God and Israel again.

Moses went back up Mount Sinai and asked God to forgive them. But if the Lord couldn't forgive them, he asked God to turn His anger against Moses. He was willing to go to hell forever to save them.

But God said no. Moses was a sinner who needed God to forgive him. He needed a sacrifice to take away his sins—he needed the promised Son of God.

When Jesus went to the cross, He stood before God. Jesus said, "Father, forgive them, for they know not what they do" (Luke 23:34). Jesus never did anything wrong, but He atoned for us by letting God punish Him on the cross. He took our place and suffered for us so God can forgive us and bring us to heaven forever.

LET'S PRAY: Lord God, I am sorry for the times I forget Your loving promises and do things that make You angry. Please forgive me for Jesus' sake, because He died on the cross in my place. In Jesus' name. Amen.

The Twelve Spies

Have you ever wanted to do something good, but your friends were too scared to join you?

Moses spent forty more days and nights on Mount Sinai while God wrote His Ten Commandments on two new stone tablets. When he came back down, the Israelites built the tent of meeting and everything that went inside.

When they were done, Moses set up the frames and curtains of the tent. Inside it, he placed the ark, the thick curtain that hid it, the lamp to light up the tent, and the gold altar for incense. Out in front, he set the bronze altar to burn sacrifices. God moved His pillar of cloud on top of the tent and filled it with His glory. Not even Moses went inside.

When it was time to go, the pillar of cloud rose from the tent. The priests covered the ark, the lamp, and the altars for the Levites to carry. The Levites took down the tent of meeting and carried it. They followed the pillar of cloud as it led them.

Finally, Israel reached the Promised Land. God told Moses to send one man from each of the twelve tribes to go into the Promised Land. They spent forty days there. The land was very good, but ten of the twelve spies didn't trust God. They told the Israelites that big, strong people were living there. They had huge cities with thick walls, and the Israelites would all be killed if they tried to go in.

But two spies trusted God and remembered His power. One was Joshua, Moses' servant. The other was Caleb from the tribe of Judah, the tribe Jesus would come from. They told the Israelites to be brave and remember how God destroyed Pharaoh's army in the Red Sea. It would be easy for God to give them the Promised Land.

But the people wouldn't listen. All night long, they cried in their tents. Then God's glory shined out from the tent of meeting. God was very, very angry at Israel. He told Moses He would destroy them because they did not trust Him or believe His promises.

But Moses prayed. He reminded the Lord of His promises to Abraham, Isaac, and Israel. He begged God to forgive His people.

God listened to Moses and did not destroy them. But since the grown-ups didn't trust God, they wouldn't enter the Promised Land. They would have to wander forty years in the wilderness. Every grown man would die there except Joshua and Caleb, who trusted God. God would give their children the Promised Land. God killed the ten unbelieving spies and sent Israel back into the wilderness.

Sometimes you need to do hard things. It is okay to be scared—just remember to pray to God and ask Him to help you do what He wants. Remind your Father in heaven He promised to help you for Jesus' sake. He will use those promises to give you courage and strong faith.

LET'S PRAY: Lord God, forgive me when I don't trust in Your promises like I should. Please make my faith strong so I may serve You with joy and peace. In Jesus' name. Amen.

Water from the Rock

Numbers 20:2–13

Do you complain a lot? What kinds of things make you want to complain?

The Israelites were not happy to spend forty years in the wilderness. They complained a lot. Moses and Aaron got tired of their griping.

Israel forgot how good and kind God had been to them. His pillar gave them shade during the day and light and warmth at night. Every day, He gave them manna. Their clothes didn't get holes in them and their sandals never wore out.

But sometimes His pillar led them through dry places where there was no water. God was testing their faith. Would they trust Him to take care of them as He promised?

Moses told us about two times this happened. The first was after they left Egypt and were going to Mount Sinai. They used up all the water they carried, and there was nothing but rocks and sand around them. They got thirsty and cranky and complained that God wasn't taking good care of them—maybe they should go back to Egypt.

That first time, God told Moses to gather Israel near a big rock, take his staff, and strike the rock with it. When he did, water came gushing out, enough for the people and all their animals.

But Israel ran out of water again. The people forgot how God brought them water out of the rock the first time. Instead, they griped and complained. Just like the first time, God told Moses to gather the Israelites around a rock. But this time, He told Moses to speak to the rock instead of hitting it. He promised water to everyone.

But Moses was tired of all the complaining and griping. He told the Israelites, "Hear now, you rebels: shall we bring water for you out of this rock?" He was so angry he took his staff and hit the rock two times, and water came gushing out.

But God was not happy with Moses. God wanted Moses to trust Him and do exactly what He said. He wanted Moses to speak to the rock, not to strike it with his staff.

Since Moses didn't do what God told him to do, God would not let Moses and Aaron lead Israel into the Promised Land.

God brought water out of the rock for the thirsty people of Israel. That water can remind you of your Baptism. God washed away your sins and made you His own child. Now Jesus leads you on the way to heaven, the land God has promised us.

Sometimes we feel like complaining about the way God takes care of us. Maybe we aren't happy with the house we have, the clothes we wear, the food we eat, the friends we have. Instead of griping and complaining, we should be glad and thank God for the wonderful gifts He gives.

LET'S PRAY: Lord God, sometimes people make me upset, and sometimes things in my life do. Forgive me for not always being kind, patient, and thankful. Help me see how good, kind, and patient You are with me—and how You gave Your Son, Jesus, to save me. In Jesus' name. Amen.

Fiery Serpents

What are some things you do when bad things happen to you?

Forty years is a long time to wander around in a desert—and to eat the same food over and over again. The Israelites were tired of eating nothing but manna.

So one more time they started griping and complaining against Moses. They really hated manna and thought it was worthless food. So the Lord sent fiery serpents into the camp. These snakes bit many people, and many died.

When the Israelites saw the serpents and people dying, they knew they should not keep complaining. They asked Moses to pray to God to take the snakes away. So Moses prayed to the Lord. But God didn't take them away; they stayed and kept biting people. Instead, He told Moses to make a bronze serpent and put it up on a pole. Then whenever the people were bitten, they could look at Moses' bronze serpent, trust the Lord's promise, and be saved from dying by God. They didn't have to do anything, just believe.

It is a great lesson. If you don't trust God's promise, the bronze serpent can't save you. But if you trust God, His promise will save you.

God used this bronze serpent on the pole to teach the Israelites one more thing about how Jesus will save us. Just as Moses lifted up the serpent on a pole, Jesus was lifted up on the cross. When we look at Jesus on the cross and believe God's promise to forgive us for Jesus' sake, we are safe. When we go through bad times and are hurting, Jesus' cross reminds us God still loves us and will make everything work out.

Moses' bronze serpent also reminds us of God's promise to Adam and Eve in the garden. When Jesus is lifted on the cross to die for us, He will crush the serpent's head, destroying Satan.

When you feel like complaining about things or when bad things happen to you, you can look to Jesus to take away your sins, to forgive you, and to help you through the hard times.

LET'S PRAY: Lord God, thank You for saving the Israelites who looked at the bronze serpent and trusted Your promise. Thank You for raising Your only Son, Jesus, on the cross. I trust Your promise to forgive me because He suffered and died in my place. In Jesus' name I pray. Amen.

Joshua Becomes Leader

Describe a bad choice you made. Did bad things happen because of that choice?

Finally, the forty long years in the desert were over. God had led Israel to the land He had promised to give Abraham, Isaac, and Jacob. They could look across the Jordan River and see it. Moses really wanted to lead them in. But he couldn't because he hit the rock in anger when God told him to talk to it. (If you forget, see "Water from the Rock," p. 257).

Moses wondered if God would change His mind and forgive him. He remembered all the times God was angry at Israel and said He would destroy them. He remembered how they worshiped the golden calf at Mount Sinai. He remembered when they refused to go into the Promised Land the first time. He remembered when they griped because they were thirsty and tired of the manna.

Each of these times, God said He was ready to destroy Israel. But Moses asked the Lord to remember His promises, and God listened to Moses and forgave them. Maybe if he asked God to forgive him for striking the rock, God would change His mind and let Moses lead Israel into the Promised Land after all.

But God answered Moses, "Enough from you; do not speak to Me of this matter again" (Deuteronomy 3:26).

The Lord had already forgiven Moses for striking the rock. But Moses had made a bad choice, and he had to live with it. God had chosen Joshua to lead Israel, and it was time for Moses to step aside.

God told Moses to take Joshua in front of the tent of meeting. As the Israelites watched, the pillar of cloud moved onto the tent of meeting. All Israel knew God had chosen Joshua to be their new leader. And they were happy with God's choice. Joshua had been Moses' helper since they left Egypt. He was with Moses on Mount Sinai when God gave him the two stone tablets with the Commandments. He was one of the good spies who told the people of Israel not to be afraid to go into the Promised Land.

While Israel was in the wilderness, several nations attacked them. Each time, Moses sent Joshua to lead Israel's army, and God always made sure Joshua won. Joshua would lead them across the Jordan River. He would lead them in battle against the nations that tried to stop them. With God's help, Joshua would give the children of Israel the land He promised to Abraham, Isaac, and Israel.

When we look at Joshua, God shows us something about Jesus, the Savior He promised to Adam and Eve. The same way Joshua would lead Israel against their enemies and give them the land God promised, Jesus will fight all our enemies and destroy them on the cross. And on the Last Day, Jesus will come back to take us to our Promised Land—our forever home with Him.

LET'S PRAY: Lord God, thank You for raising up Joshua to lead the people of Israel into the Promised Land. Thank You for raising up Jesus to lead us through this life. We know He will come back to bring us to live with You. In Jesus' name. Amen.

Who is the oldest person you know? How strong and healthy is he or she?

Moses was 120 years old, but he was just as strong as when he was young. Think about all the things God did through Moses. He used ten plagues to lead Israel out of Egypt. He parted the waters of the Red Sea and let Israel cross on dry ground. He guided the people to Mount Sinai, where they received God's Commandments. He told the workers how to build the ark of the covenant and the tent of meeting, where they could offer sacrifices for their sins. He led them to the Promised Land twice. Many times, he asked God to forgive Israel when the Lord was angry and ready to destroy them.

But Moses' work was all done. God had made Joshua the new leader to bring Israel into the Promised Land. Before Moses died, he gathered Israel together and gave them one last good-bye sermon. He wrote it down in the book we call Deuteronomy (dew-tuh-RON-uh-mee).

After that, God told Moses to climb a high mountain called Mount Nebo (NEE-boh). From the top, God showed him the Promised Land and where each tribe would live. Then Moses died on the mountain.

Moses was all alone when he died. So God took care of burying his body.

Of all the people we will meet in the Old Testament, no one was like Moses. God worked more miracles through him than any person until Jesus came. In fact, in his last good-bye message, Moses made a great promise: "The LORD your God will raise up for you a prophet like me from among you, from your brothers— it is to Him you shall listen" (Deuteronomy 18:15). He was talking about Jesus.

Like Moses, Jesus taught us all about God. Like Moses, Jesus did great powerful works— healing the sick, driving out demons, raising the dead, making storms stop, and walking on water.

Jesus was like Moses in another way too. When God was angry at Israel for their sins, Moses begged God to forgive them and even offered to take their place. Jesus really did take our place when He went to the cross and died to save us from our sins.

Like Moses, Jesus died. But unlike Moses, Jesus didn't stay dead. Three days after He died on the cross, Jesus rose again, and now He is always with us to teach us, protect us, and guide us to His promised land. On the day Jesus returns, He will raise Moses' body, and we will be able to meet him.

God has a plan for you too. As you study His Bible, go to church and Sunday School, and pray, He will lead you to do wonderful, important things for Him. These things may not be as big and flashy as what Moses did, but through your words and the things you do, Jesus will show many people just how much God loves them and how Jesus died to save them. That is exciting!

LET'S PRAY: Lord God, thank You for raising up Moses to free Your people from slavery. But even more, thank You for raising Jesus to set us free from sin, death, and hell. Now raise me up to love other people and help them learn about Jesus. In Jesus' name. Amen.

Rahab Hides the Spies Joshua 2

What is the scariest thing you have ever done?

Moses was dead, and Joshua was now Israel's leader. Across the Jordan River, he saw an important city called Jericho (JER-ih-koh). It blocked the way into the Promised Land and was protected by a huge, strong wall.

Joshua sent two spies to go into the city, see how strong its walls were, and report on how the soldiers guarded it. They sneaked inside and went into the house of a woman named Rahab (RAY-hab).

But someone told the king of Jericho that Israelite spies were hiding in Rahab's house. He sent soldiers to capture them. The soldiers told Rahab to bring out the men.

This could have been really scary for the spies. Bad things would have happened if Rahab handed them over to the king. But bad things didn't happen. Rahab believed in the Lord, the God of Israel. When she learned the men were spies, she took them onto her roof and told them to hide behind some plants stacked up there.

Then she told the soldiers the men had been there before, but they had gone out before the gate closed for the night. The soldiers rushed out to search for them.

After the soldiers left, Rahab went back to the spies on the roof. She told them everyone in Jericho was scared of God. They were talking about how He had dried up the Red Sea so the Israelites could pass through on dry land but sent the waters back down on the Egyptians. That had happened forty years before, but the people of Jericho still remembered and were really scared. They were also scared after hearing about the battles the Israelites had won on the other side of the Jordan River.

Rahab knew God would give the Promised Land to Israel. So she asked the spies to protect her and her family the same way she was protecting them. They gave her a red cord and told her to tie it in her window. When the Israelites saw it, they would protect her and everyone in the house with her.

She let the spies down by a rope from that window, and they returned safely to the Israelite camp. They told Joshua and the Israelites about Rahab and how everyone in Jericho was scared of them. The whole camp was glad and praised God.

God was looking out for both Rahab and the spies that day. He led them to her so she could protect them and they could protect her. The Israelites kept their promise, and Rahab and her family were saved.

Later, Rahab married an Israelite who was in the line that led from Adam and Eve to God's promised Savior. Rahab and her husband had a baby boy who was in that line too, the line that ended with God's Son, our Lord Jesus.

Sometimes we have to do things that are really scary. But God is always with us, and He can even bring us friends who will help and protect us.

LET'S PRAY: Lord God, Your powerful deeds made the people of Jericho tremble in fear. Thank You that we do not need to be afraid of You, because Jesus, our Savior, took our place on the cross. Help us tell others about His great love. We pray in Jesus' name. Amen.

Entering the Promised Land Joshua 3–4

Do you ever pick up seashells, rocks, or other things to take home to remind you of a wonderful place?

It was time for Israel to cross the Jordan River into the land God promised to give to Abraham, Isaac, and Israel. Joshua commanded the priests, the children and grandchildren of Moses' brother, Aaron, to carry the ark of the covenant to the riverbank. Joshua told the people of Israel to follow the ark. But they should not come close to it. They needed to stay far away, on the left and the right sides of the ark.

But there was a problem. That time of the year was the rainy season. The Jordan River was flooding out of its banks. Anyone who stepped into the water would get knocked over by the water and swept away. This probably made the king of Jericho feel a little safer. At least during this rainy season, the Israelite army should not be able to come over and fight them.

The priests walked right up to the edge of the water, but would they trust God enough to step down into that flooded river?

Almost forty years before, God promised their fathers He would protect them and give them the Promised Land. But their fathers did not trust Him. They stayed in their tents crying and griping and complaining.

But these Israelites were different. The Holy Spirit had given them strong faith, and they trusted God's Word.

The priests boldly stepped down into the rushing river, and God cut off the waters. The waters gathered together very far upstream. The riverbed where the priests stood should have been thick mud, but it had instantly become dry ground. They carried the ark out to the middle of the river and stood still.

The Israelites began crossing on both sides of the ark, right in front of Jericho.

Joshua commanded twelve men, one from each tribe, to go to the place where the priests were standing with the ark. Each man picked up a rock from there. They carried their twelve rocks over to the shore and set them down. Joshua set these up as a memorial.

Whenever Israelites would come back to visit that place, especially the children, they would know those were the very same rocks that were in the Jordan River where the ark stood as the Israelites crossed into the Promised Land.

When all Israel was across, the priests came up out of the river and stepped onto the shore. Right away, God released the water, and it roared down the riverbed again, returning to flood stage.

The king of Jericho saw this and lost all his courage. What walls could stand against the God of Israel?

God likes us to remember the good things He has done for us. That is why we celebrate Christmas year after year. We also spend time each year to remember Jesus' death on the cross and His rising to life again.

LET'S PRAY: Lord, our God, thank You for using Your mighty power to dry up the Jordan River so Your people could cross over into the Promised Land. Thank You for Jesus, who has brought us over from death to life through His life, death, and resurrection. In Jesus' name. Amen.

The Walls of Jericho

When you were really little, where was your favorite place to hide when you were scared? Does it feel safe now?

The people of Jericho were very scared. God's people had crossed the Jordan River and were camped right outside their city. The people of Jericho locked all the city gates and hid behind the thick walls that towered high over their heads. They hoped these walls would be strong enough to keep out the Israelites.

God told Joshua to gather all his men together and march them around the city one time. They were to be careful not to say a word.

In the middle of the army, Joshua lined up seven priests. They walked side by side, each blowing a ram's horn like a trumpet. Behind this line followed other priests who carried the ark.

The Israelite army walked around the city one time, trumpets blowing, and then returned to camp.

The next day, the Israelites did the same. And the next day. And the next day. For six days, the Israelites walked around the city one time, trumpets blasting. Then they returned to camp.

On the seventh day, the Israelite army gathered at sunrise and began marching around the city. But this time, they didn't stop after one time around. They circled it a second time and a third and a fourth. They kept going around a fifth time and a sixth time.

Finally, the Israelites walked around the city a seventh time. Then Joshua gave a command. The priests blew their trumpets, and from every direction around the city a loud roar rose as the Israelites all shouted with mighty voices.

The people of Jericho watched in terror as the mighty walls of their city crumbled and fell all around them. The Israelites marched straight up into the city and captured it.

The spies who hid in Rahab's house went and brought her and her family out. They led her family safely out of the city and then burned it with fire. Rahab and her family lived with the people of Israel and worshiped their God.

The people of Jericho hid behind their mighty walls, hoping they could keep God out. But no hiding place can keep Him away.

But we don't need to be scared or try to hide away from God the way the people of Jericho did, the way Adam and Eve did. Jesus died on the cross for us, and our Baptism is like that scarlet cord tied in Rahab's window. When Jesus comes back, He will lead us out of this world and bring us home to live with Him forever.

LET'S PRAY: Lord, no thick walls are strong enough to keep You out. Come into my heart and guide me so I can tell others about the great things You've done for us, especially how Jesus came to this world as one of the children of Rahab and saved all of us from our sins. In Jesus' name. Amen.

When was the last time you needed someone's help?

After Jericho's walls fell, God sent Israel to punish the other nations living in the Promised Land for not believing when Abraham taught them about the true God. In the south, five kings joined their armies together and went to fight Joshua. But God threw huge hailstones down on them. The scared men turned and started running back to their strong cities. Israel chased after them, but Joshua saw the armies would get away when it got dark. So he asked God to make the sun stand still in the sky—and God did. Not one of those men got back to their homes.

When the kings in the north learned what happened, they joined together to form an even bigger army to fight against Israel. But God gave them to Joshua too. When the fighting was all over, Joshua divided up the land between the twelve tribes of Israel.

After Joshua died, the people forgot about the good things the Lord had done and His promise to send the Savior. They served the false gods of the nations around them. So God brought nations in that treated the Israelites badly. Then the Israelites asked God to help them, and God raised up leaders called judges who set them free.

For twenty years, Israel had suffered under a king named Jabin (JAY-bin) and his army leader named Sisera (SIS-uh-rah). Israel prayed to God for help, and God sent a message to a woman named Deborah. She told an Israelite fighter named Barak (BAIR-uhk) that God wanted him to go fight against Sisera.

But Barak told Deborah he would not go to fight unless she went with him, so she went. But since he didn't trust God enough to go without her, she told him he wouldn't be the one to beat Sisera—a woman would.

Barak's army attacked Sisera's army and destroyed it. That scared Sisera. He jumped off his chariot and ran away to hide in the tent of his king's friend. This friend wanted to help Sisera's king, but his wife, Jael (JAY-uhl), loved God and wanted to help His people. She smiled and told Sisera not to be afraid, but to come on inside her tent. She covered him with a rug and gave him some milk to drink. He was so tired that he fell fast asleep. While Sisera slept, Jael killed him. She went out of her tent and saw Barak searching for Sisera. She told him, "Come, and I will show you the man you are seeking." When he went inside the tent, he found Sisera lying dead. God had raised up Deborah and Jael to free Israel again.

There are times in your life when you will need help. Pray to God, and He will raise people up to help you too. But remember, sometimes you will be the person He raises up to help someone else.

Gideon the Coward

Describe a time when you comforted a friend who was scared.

After Deborah died, the people started serving other gods again. God wanted to bring them back to Him, so He brought in a country called Midian (MID-ee-uhn). Every time the Israelites planted food, the Midianites brought in their animals to eat up all that food. When they saw the Midianites coming, God's people left their homes and hid in caves and up in the mountains. It got so bad the Israelites turned back to God and asked Him for help.

This time God chose a man named Gideon (GIH-dee-uhn) to be the next judge. By himself, Gideon was way too scared to save Israel. So God's angel came and promised him the Lord would be with him.

Gideon called the Israelites to come fight with him against the Midianites. But he was still afraid. So he asked God to show him a miracle to make him braver. He laid a fleece on the ground and asked God to let dew fall just on the fleece and let everything else be dry. He knew dew usually covered everything, even clothes and hair. When he went outside the next morning, the ground was dry, but the fleece was soaking wet.

But Gideon was still not sure. He asked God to do the same thing the next night—but this time let the fleece be dry and everything else wet. And God did that too. So Gideon went to war.

Midianites were spread out all over the land, too many to count. Only 32,000 Israelite soldiers were brave enough to come with Gideon. But God told him that was way too many men—they would think they won the battle themselves. So Gideon sent home everyone who was too scared to fight. Only 10,000 were left, but God said that was still too many people. God chose 300 soldiers for Gideon.

God told Gideon to have his 300 men go out to the Midianites. In the middle of the night, they stood outside the Midianite camp. In one hand, they held a jar with a torch inside; in the other hand, they held a trumpet. When Gideon gave a signal, they broke the pots so their torches shone brightly. Then they shouted, "A sword for the Lord and for Gideon!" Each stood in his place, holding his torch and blowing his trumpet. The Midianites woke up confused, like they were in the middle of a nightmare. In the darkness, they started swinging their swords wildly. They hit only one another before they ran away in fright. Without using a single weapon from the Israelite army, God had saved His people.

Like Gideon, sometimes we are asked to do things that seem very, very scary. But God promises to be with us no matter what. In Jesus, He has given us the victory.

LET'S PRAY: Lord, thank You for choosing a scared young man to be judge. Thank You for showing us that You are our strong defender and helper. Most of all, thank You for sending Jesus to conquer sin, death, Satan, and hell all by Himself, without needing any help from us. We pray with confidence in Jesus' name. Amen.

Samson the Strongman

What would you do if you were the strongest person in the world?

After Gideon died, Israel turned away from God again. God brought in a strong people called the Philistines (fih-LISS-teenz). The Israelites suffered so much that they prayed to God for help. God sent the Angel of the Lord to an Israelite woman. He told her she would have a baby boy and the hair on his head must never be cut. The angel said, "He will begin to save Israel from the hand of the Philistines." She named her baby Samson.

Samson grew up, and God gave him great strength. Once he killed a lion with his bare hands. But Samson didn't want to help Israel; he only did things that made him feel happy. But then the Philistines did things that made him mad, so he burned the crops in their fields and killed many Philistines. Then he went to hide in a small cave in the mountains of Israel.

The Philistines came into the mountains to find him. The Israelites were scared, so they tied up Samson and handed him over to the Philistines. But the Spirit of God rushed upon Samson. The ropes melted off his arms, and he killed one thousand Philistines.

Sometime later, Samson loved a beautiful Philistine woman named Delilah (dee-LIGH-lah). The Philistine rulers promised to give her a lot of silver if she learned how to make Samson lose his strength. Over and over, Delilah asked Samson to tell her his secret. Whenever he wouldn't tell her, she cried and said he didn't love her. Finally, she wore him out and Samson said, "If my head is shaved, then my strength will leave me." While Samson slept on her lap, a man sneaked in and cut off his hair. The Holy Spirit left Samson, and the Philistines caught him. They made him blind and put him in prison. But Samson's hair started growing again.

One day, all the important Philistines gathered in the temple of their god Dagon (DAY-gahn) to thank him for helping them capture Samson. They brought Samson out to make fun of him. Samson asked a young man to lead him to the two pillars that held up the roof. Leaning against the pillars, he prayed, "O Lord God, please remember me and please strengthen me only this once." Samson pushed with all his might. The pillars snapped, the roof fell down, and many, many Philistine rulers were killed. Samson died too. His brothers came and buried his body.

God has given you special gifts too. Maybe you are really good at math, science, or English. Maybe you are good at sports, music, or dancing. Maybe you are a good friend and listener. Like Samson, you can be selfish and use those gifts only to make yourself happy. But God gave you those gifts to help other people. With the power of the Holy Spirit, you can do great things too.

LET'S PRAY: Lord God, Samson was horribly selfish and wasted the great power You gave him. But when he was in prison, You brought him back to You. Thank You for the gifts You gave me. Teach me not to be selfish but to use Your gifts to show other people Your great love. In Jesus' name. Amen.

God Calls Samuel

1 Samuel 1; 3

What is it like to play with someone who wants to make all the rules?

Samson was dead, but most Israelites were just like he was. They didn't care about God or helping one another. They wanted only to do what felt right to them. That made life really hard and sad.

God raised up one last judge. He chose a woman named Hannah to be his mother. Hannah was married but couldn't have a baby. So she went to the tabernacle and prayed, "If You give to Your servant a son, then I will give him to the Lord all the days of his life, and no razor shall touch his head." Just like Samson, he would be a Nazirite. When her baby was born, Hannah named him Samuel. When Samuel was still young, Hannah kept her promise and brought him to the tabernacle. Samuel stayed there and grew up with the high priest named Eli.

One night, young Samuel heard a voice call, "Samuel, Samuel." He climbed out of bed, ran to Eli, and said, "Here I am, for you called me." But Eli said, "I didn't call you" and sent him back to bed.

Again the voice called, Samuel went to Eli, and Eli sent him back to bed. When the voice called a third time, Eli realized God was calling Samuel. He told Samuel what to say if his name was called again, and he sent him to lay back down.

When God called again, Samuel answered, "Speak, Lord, for Your servant hears." The Lord told Samuel He would punish Eli's two grownup sons who were priests. They had been breaking His commands in front of the Israelites. Eli would also die, because he was their father and didn't stop them.

When Samuel woke up the next morning, Eli asked him what God said. Samuel was afraid, but told Eli everything. Eli said, "It is the Lord. Let Him do what seems good to Him."

Shortly after that, the Israelites fought the Philistines. God let the Philistines win. When Eli learned they had killed his sons and captured the ark of the covenant, he got so upset he fell over backward in his chair and died.

The Philistines carried God's ark into the temple of their god, Dagon. But when they came the next morning, Dagon's statue had fallen on its face before the ark. They set the statue back up. The next morning, Dagon had fallen again—but this time his hands and head were broken off. God was showing the Philistines Dagon was not real and had no power to help them.

The longer the Philistines kept the ark, the more God hurt them. So they sent it back to God's people, where it belonged.

Samuel grew up to be a powerful prophet and a good judge for God's people.

Samuel was pretty young when God first talked to him. No matter how young you are, you can pray to God and hear Him speak to you through His words in the Bible. Like God did great things through Samuel, God wants to do great things for His people through you.

LET'S PRAY: Lord God, thank You for leading Your people through Samuel. Help me love listening to Your words too, so I can serve You and Your people all my life. In Jesus' name. Amen.

89

Have you ever had to do something that seemed way too hard to do?

Samuel was a good judge and prophet, but his sons ended up being just as bad as Eli's sons had been. The Israelites didn't want Samuel's evil sons ruling them after he died, so they told him to give them a king like every other nation had.

Samuel didn't want to do this. God was Israel's King. But the people of Israel were stubborn. All the other nations had a king, so they wanted one too. God told Samuel to give them a king like they asked. Here is where we see how wonderful God is. He could have been mad and given them a really bad king. But He loved His people and chose a really good man to be their first king.

Saul was that man. He lived in the tribe of Benjamin. One day, his father's donkeys ran away. His father sent him to go look for them. Saul took a servant along, and they looked all over for them, but they didn't have any luck. Saul's servant told him they should go and ask Samuel. Samuel told Saul he would find the donkeys. But more important, he told him God had chosen him to be king over Israel. Saul was a very shy man who didn't think he was able to be king.

But Samuel poured oil on Saul's head. Later, the Holy Spirit rushed upon him. With the Holy Spirit upon him, Saul had the courage and everything else he would ever need to be a great king, to serve God and His people all his life.

Samuel gathered all Israel together to show them the man God had chosen to be their king. Out of the twelve tribes gathered there, God chose Benjamin. Out of all the families in the tribe of Benjamin, God picked Saul's family. And from all the people in Saul's family, God chose Saul. But Saul was nowhere to be seen.

God told Samuel that Saul was hiding among the bags. Samuel found him and brought him out to the people. When they saw Saul, they were really excited—he was big and tall like they thought a king should be.

During his first years as king, Saul loved God and cared about God's people very much. He was very brave and courageous and fought hard against the Philistines. His son Jonathan was especially brave because he loved and trusted God.

When God baptized you, He did something like what He did to Saul. When water was poured on your head, God washed away all your sins and made you His own child for Jesus' sake. The Holy Spirit was given to you, and with the Holy Spirit you now have everything you need to be a child of God, to serve Him and His people all your life.

LET'S PRAY: Lord God, when Your people rejected You as their King, You still loved them. You sent Your own Son, Jesus, to be King and save us all by dying on the cross and rising to life again. Thank You for sending Your Holy Spirit upon me too. In Jesus' name. Amen.

God Rejects Saul and Chooses David
1 Samuel 15–16

Describe someone who ended up being very different from who you first thought this person would be.

During his first years, Saul was a good king. He was humble and did everything Samuel told him God wanted him to do. But after a while, Saul became proud. He forgot Israel belonged to God and thought it was his country to rule as he wanted. God gave him important jobs, but Saul wasn't careful to do everything the way God told him to do it.

Since Saul wasn't obeying God, Samuel told him the Lord would take the kingdom away from him and give it to a man who put God first. The Holy Spirit left Saul, and an evil spirit went into him. It made Saul feel really bad, and he didn't know how to make it go away so he could feel better.

Samuel was really sad and upset. He loved Saul and prayed for God to give the king another chance. But God had made up His mind. He told Samuel to stop feeling sorry. He was to go to the little town of Bethlehem and anoint one of the sons of a man named Jesse (JEH-see) to be king.

Samuel went to Bethlehem and prepared a sacrifice. Everyone from the town gathered, and Samuel met Jesse and his sons. Jesse's oldest son, Eliab (ih-LIGH-ab), was grown up and very tall and handsome. Samuel thought this must be the new king God had chosen. But God told Samuel not to look at how tall and handsome Eliab was. God had looked inside his heart and didn't want him to be the next king.

Samuel met the rest of Jesse's sons, but God did not choose any of them. Samuel asked, "Are all your sons here?" Jesse told him there was still the youngest son, but he was watching the sheep. Samuel said, "Send and get him, for we will not sit down till he comes here."

Then Jesse's youngest son, David, came in from the field. Samuel saw that he was not grown up yet, but he was very handsome. The Lord told Samuel, "Anoint him." So Samuel took oil and poured it on David's head. Immediately, the Holy Spirit rushed upon David.

King Saul was still feeling bad. A servant told him about one of Jesse's sons who was very good at playing music. Saul told Jesse to send David to play for him. Whenever David played his harp, the evil spirit left Saul and he felt better.

It is easy for us to look at someone new and think we can guess what kind of person he or she is. But what we see on the outside is often different from the real person inside. Ask God to open your eyes and help you get to know every person as he or she really is. Ask Him to help you be a friend and show each person God's love.

LET'S PRAY: Lord God, You sent Samuel to Bethlehem, the town where Jesus, Your Son, would be born. And there You chose David to be the next king after Saul. Make me strong in faith, that I may serve You by taking care of others. In Jesus' name. Amen.

David and Goliath

Who is the biggest, meanest kid at school?

David's three oldest brothers were in King Saul's army fighting against the Philistines. Every morning and evening for forty days, a huge Philistine named Goliath stepped forward and shouted at the Israelites. He was a powerful warrior who stood over nine feet tall. He challenged Israel to send one warrior to fight with him one on one. King Saul should have gone to fight him, but he was afraid and did not trust God anymore. None of his soldiers were brave enough either.

But on the fortieth day, David came into the camp. His father sent him to bring his brothers food and find out how they were doing. David listened to what Goliath shouted at the Israelites, and he got really, really mad. Goliath was making fun of God! If no other Israelite was brave enough to fight Goliath, David would go. He was not afraid.

King Saul found out and called for him. But when Saul saw that David was just a boy, he said, "You are not able to go against this Philistine to fight with him, for you are but a youth."

David told King Saul what he did as a shepherd. Whenever a lion or a bear would attack his sheep, David would never run away. He always ran after it to hit it and kill it. David told Saul, "The Lord who delivered me from the paw of the lion and from the paw of the bear will deliver me from the hand of this Philistine."

Goliath stood behind his shield, dressed in his armor. He held his sword in his huge hand. Saul wanted David to wear his armor, but Saul was much taller than David and so his armor was way too big for David to walk in. David went to fight Goliath just as he was.

When Goliath realized David was just a boy, he made fun of him. David told him, "This day the Lord will deliver you into my hand, and I will strike you down."

David pulled a stone out of his pouch and put it in his sling. He swung the sling around, twirling it faster and faster. Then he let go of one strap and the stone shot out, hit Goliath on the forehead, and knocked him flat onto the ground. David ran up, grabbed the giant's sword, and killed him with it.

When the Philistine army saw their hero dead, they turned and ran away in fear. The soldiers of Israel shouted and started chasing after them.

King Saul thought David was too young to fight against Goliath. Maybe people think you are too young to do great things for God. But God is the one who gives His people power to do great things—whether they are young or old. Be bold and trust God like David did, and God will do great things through you too.

LET'S PRAY: Lord God, give me the same faith and courage You gave David, that I may not fear any person but know that You are always with me, no matter what. Thank You for David's victory, and also for Your Son, Jesus, who went to the cross to destroy an even greater giant, Satan. I pray in Jesus' name. Amen.

David, Jonathan, and Saul

What are some things you can do if someone is being mean to you?

After David killed Goliath, King Saul had him come and live in his house. David loved King Saul and fought hard to protect and help him. Saul had a son named Jonathan. Jonathan was brave like David. He loved God and did great things with God's help. When Jonathan saw David kill Goliath, he and David became best friends.

When David went out to fight for Saul, God helped him beat the Philistines over and over. The people loved David and sang songs about him. That made Saul jealous and angry. He wanted to be the one they sang about. He started to think David would try to kill him and take his place as king.

That feeling got even worse when the evil spirit came on Saul. David played his harp to make Saul feel better, but once Saul threw his spear at David to kill him. David got away, and Jonathan went to talk to his dad. He told Saul there was no reason to be afraid of David—he should be thanking him instead. David killed Goliath when everyone else was too scared to fight him. David fought hard to help Saul beat the Philistines. Saul listened to Jonathan this time.

But Saul kept thinking that David was only pretending to love him. He thought David was really waiting for a chance to kill him. When Jonathan tried to defend David again, Saul became angry and tried to kill Jonathan too.

Jonathan was really upset that his father was treating David so badly. He told David he needed to run away or Saul would kill him. The two friends hugged each other and cried. David went up into the mountains and hid in caves. Jonathan visited David in the mountains too. He helped David find strength in God's promises. He knew David would be the next king, and he wanted to be at his side to help him.

King Saul brought the army of Israel into the mountains to hunt for David to kill him. Two times David had the chance to kill Saul, but he let him go because God had anointed Saul as king. David would not take the throne until God chose to give it to him.

Finally, the Philistines came up against Israel, and Saul had to fight them without David's help. The Philistines fought so hard that Saul's men ran away in fear. Jonathan stayed to fight and was killed. Saul got badly hurt and killed himself in the battle. When David heard the news, he was very, very sad.

God protected David and kept him safe from King Saul. But even though Saul mistreated David, David still respected him and saved his life because God had chosen Saul to be king. God chose people and gave them to us as our parents, our pastors, and our teachers. We honor God when we support them, treat them with respect, and pray for them, even when we don't like them.

LET'S PRAY: Lord God, help me to never be jealous and angry like King Saul, but to love and trust You like David and Jonathan did. Thank You for the friends You have given me. Help me to be as good a friend to them as Jonathan and David were to each other. I pray in the name of Jesus, my best friend of all. Amen.

God's Covenant with David

If you were to build a new church, what would you want it to look like?

After King Saul died in battle, David became king over the twelve tribes of Israel. He fought many dangerous battles to defend Israel from their enemies. God was with him and helped him win every time. David captured a high, strong city called Jerusalem and made it his new home. He brought the ark of the covenant up into it. The Israelites called it the city of David.

Finally, a time came when the enemies stopped rising up against Israel, and David had peace. He built a fine house to live in. But then he thought about God's ark. He felt bad knowing he was in this nice house while the ark was still in a tent. Israel was at peace, and the ark did not have to move around anymore. David thought, "God is so great and wonderful; shouldn't He have a house that is great and wonderful too?"

David called the prophet Nathan (NAY-thuhn) and told him he wanted to build a great and beautiful temple to hold the ark of God, a much nicer place than the tabernacle.

At first, Nathan agreed. He knew the Spirit of God was in David because Samuel had anointed him, and he thought God was telling David to build it. But that night, God came to Nathan and told him to go back and talk to David. Nathan told the king God did not want him to build His temple. David had fought in many, many wars. He wanted David's son Solomon to build it because Israel would be at peace all the time Solomon was king.

But Nathan said that God wanted to build something for David. "The Lord will make you a house." After David's work was finished and he died, God would raise up one of David's offspring to reign in David's place. This Son of David would be king forever.

David knew God wasn't talking about his son Solomon anymore. God was talking about the Savior He had first promised to Adam and Eve in the garden, and then to Abraham, Isaac, and Jacob—Jesus Christ, God's Son. Now David knew the Savior would come from his own family. He was very happy and wondered why God had chosen him. David knew he was a sinner like all of us and didn't deserve to be in the line that would lead to the coming Savior.

When Jesus was on earth, people called Him the Son of David. That meant they believed Jesus was the Savior God had promised long ago.

One day, you may help build a church where people can come together and learn all about Jesus. But even better, Jesus promised us He is building a wonderful house for us in heaven. And on the Last Day, He will come back to take us to live with Him forever.

LET'S PRAY: Lord God, thank You for choosing David to be one of those through whom Jesus would come. Give me a strong faith and trust in Jesus, my Savior, as I wait to see the house He is getting ready for me in heaven. In Jesus' name. Amen.

The Wisdom of Solomon 1 Kings 3

If you could ask for anything in the whole world, what would you ask for?

David ruled as king over Israel's twelve tribes for nearly forty years. He had many wives and many children from those wives. When the time came close for him to die, David chose his young son Solomon to be the next king. David must have told Solomon to pray and study God's Word so that he could be strong and walk in the ways of the Lord (see 1 Kings 2). Then David died.

Solomon then became king over the twelve tribes of Israel. He loved God and was careful to follow his father David's instructions. One night after Solomon made many, many sacrifices, God appeared to him in a dream. The Lord told him, "Ask what I shall give you."

What would you do if God told you to ask what He should give you? Solomon could have been selfish and asked for lots of money. He could have asked for a long life, or he could have asked God to kill all his enemies. Instead, he thought about the people who needed him. He thought how hard it was to be a king and how young he was. He knew he had a lot to learn, and he would have to make some really tough decisions. So he asked God to give him an understanding mind so he could clearly know what was right and what was wrong and lead Israel the way God wanted him to lead them.

God was very happy with Solomon's answer because the young man wanted to please God and take good care of the people of Israel. He could have asked for something for himself, but he didn't. He wanted something that would help him lead God's people better. So God gave Solomon the understanding mind he asked for, and God gave him great wisdom.

No puzzle or riddle was too hard for Solomon to understand. He could listen to two people and figure out who was lying and who was telling the truth. He knew how to make good decisions and do the things that were best for God's people. Before long, people were coming from all around the world to talk to Solomon, to ask him questions, and to offer him wonderful gifts.

As you grow up, there are many things you could want and work hard to get. But it is better to help your neighbors and friends than to help yourself. Just like Solomon, remember to be strong and walk in God's ways, which we learn as we read the Bible and pray. And because of Jesus, you can be bold to ask God to make you wise and help you learn to become better at using the gifts He gave you when He baptized you. He gave you those gifts so you can use them to help your family and friends and to build up His Church.

LET'S PRAY: Lord God, thank You for giving Solomon the gift of an understanding mind so he could make good decisions. Please give me wisdom too, so I know how to live my life and help the people around me. In Jesus' name. Amen.

Solomon Builds the Temple

Think of the way your church is built. What does it tell you about God?

The time came to build God's temple—a beautiful building that would show the world Israel's great God lived with His people. It was laid out like the tabernacle. Both had two rooms inside and a large courtyard outside where God's people gathered. They listened to God's words and called on Him with their prayers, hymns, and songs. Outside the temple, Solomon placed the altar where the animal sacrifices were burned.

The inside of the temple was a lot like our churches today, but none of the Israelites were allowed to go inside, only the priests and Levites. It had two rooms. The first room was called the Holy Place. Here, Solomon placed a table for burning incense and a beautiful golden lampstand. Every morning and afternoon, the people watched the priests go inside to burn incense while they prayed outside. After he offered the incense, the priest came out and said words you hear in church: "The LORD bless you and keep you; the LORD make His face to shine upon you and be gracious to you; the LORD lift up His countenance upon you and give you peace" (Numbers 6:24–26).

Hanging between this front room and the next was a curtain. Behind it was the special room called the Most Holy Place. Two huge angels stood in this room, spreading their wings over the ark of the covenant and the two angels on its cover. Only the high priest could come into this room one day each year—the Day of Atonement. He would bring blood from sacrificed animals and sprinkle it on the ark so God could forgive the Israelites' sins.

Solomon gathered all Israel together, and the priests carried the ark into the temple. Suddenly a bright cloud filled the temple. God's people saw He was in the temple, right there among His people.

Everything in the temple teaches us something about Jesus, our great High Priest. Just like God came among the people in the cloud that filled the temple, Jesus came to live among us when He came down from heaven and was born as a little baby. The Day of Atonement pointed ahead to Good Friday, when Jesus died on the cross to take away our sins. Like the high priest, Jesus offered His blood so God His Father could forgive all our sins. When Jesus died on the cross, the curtain was torn in two from top to bottom. That showed that Jesus opened the way for us to come to God our Father and pray to Him.

LET'S PRAY: Almighty God, thank You for the temple, which reminded Your people You were right there with them all the time. Thank You also for my church, which reminds me You are always here to hear my prayers. Help me always love coming to Your church to hear Your Word, give You my thanks and praise, and one day receive Holy Communion. In Jesus' name. Amen.

103

Jeroboam and the Divided Kingdom

1 Kings 11–12

Do you listen more to your friends or to your parents and teachers?

When Solomon was young, he loved God and built the great temple. But when he got older, he thought it would be smart to marry princesses from other countries. He thought that would keep their fathers, who were kings, from attacking Israel and maybe hurting their daughters. Solomon should have trusted God to protect Israel instead. These princesses believed in many false gods, and since Solomon loved them more than he loved God, he built temples to their gods in Jerusalem.

God was angry that Solomon had turned away from Him and led Israel to turn away too. He decided to take the kingdom away from Solomon's son. But since He promised to send the Savior from David's line, God decided not to take every tribe away from David. David's family would keep the tribe of Judah (called the Southern Kingdom or Judah, although it also included Simeon and part of Benjamin). But God would give ten tribes to another man.

Solomon died, and his son Rehoboam (ray-oh-BOH-uhm) became king. One of the leaders of Solomon's workers was named Jeroboam (jer-uh-BOH-uhm). He promised Rehoboam the Israelites would serve him if he didn't make them work as hard for him as they had to work for Solomon.

Rehoboam asked the older people who served his father what he should do. They gave him good advice. They told him the people would serve him if he did what they asked. But Rehoboam didn't like what they said. He was too proud and wanted to show the people he was strong. He asked his young friends, and they told him to act tough. Rehoboam told Jeroboam he would make Israel work even harder than his father, Solomon, had made them work.

The other tribes got so mad they left and made Jeroboam their king. Rehoboam gathered his soldiers to go and fight against them. But God told him not to fight—God had divided Israel into two kingdoms. Rehoboam obeyed God and let the other tribes leave. We call those other tribes the Northern Kingdom or Israel.

Jeroboam was a strong king, but he didn't trust God. He was afraid his people would want to leave him and return to the house of David when they went up to worship God in the Jerusalem temple. So he made two golden calves and set one up in the northern part of his kingdom and the other in the southern part. This made God angry because the people of the Northern Kingdom turned away from Him to these false gods who could not help them.

As you grow up, you will make important decisions. One of the most important is whom you will listen to—to God or to your friends? Solomon listened to his wives, Rehoboam listened to his friends, and Jeroboam listened to his fears. Learn from their mistakes and listen to God. You will see God is the only one worth trusting.

LET'S PRAY: Lord God, it is so sad to see how many times the people of Israel and their kings turned away from You. But we also are quick to listen to other people and not to You. Please forgive us for Jesus' sake and make us strong in faith so we love and trust You alone, because You gave Your Son to save us. In Jesus' name. Amen.

Elijah and the Prophets of Baal

What is something amazing God could do to show He is real?

God divided the twelve tribes into two kingdoms: Judah in the south and Israel in the north. The worst king in the north was named Ahab (AY-hab). He married a woman named Jezebel (JEZ-uh-bel). She was a princess from another kingdom and was very, very bad. She taught Ahab to worship her god named Baal (BAY-uhl). Jezebel killed God's prophets and made the people of Israel worship Baal.

Just when the Northern Kingdom was as far away from God as it could be, the Lord sent a great prophet named Elijah (ih-LIGH-jah) to bring His people back. Elijah told King Ahab, "There shall be no dew or rain these years, except by my word." And it stopped raining. Food wouldn't grow in the fields, and the animals couldn't stay alive.

Finally, after three-and-a-half years, God told Elijah to go back to King Ahab and gather the people together at a place called Mount Carmel. They would have a big contest to prove who was the real God—Baal or the Lord God. Elijah was the only prophet of God, but Baal had 450 prophets.

Baal's prophets built an altar, put wood down, and then put a bull on it. Then they prayed to Baal to set the wood on fire—but nothing happened. They shouted and danced around wildly, but still no fire. They even cut themselves with knives to get Baal's attention but nothing happened—because Baal was not real.

Then, late in the afternoon, Elijah told the people to come near. He set up an altar with twelve large stones—one for each of the twelve tribes of Israel. He laid out the wood, set the bull on the altar, and dug a deep trench around it. He told men to fill four jars full of water and

pour them over the meat and the wood. He told them to pour water a second time, then a third time. The wood was soaking wet and water filled the trenches.

Then Elijah prayed, and the Lord God sent fire down from heaven. It burned up the meat, the wood, the stones, all the water, and even the dirt! The people shouted, "The Lord, He is God! The Lord, He is God!"

Elijah told King Ahab God was going to send rain, so he had better get into his chariot and race home before the rain came. Then the Spirit of God came on Elijah. He ran to the same town faster than King Ahab's horses could run.

God's love for you is just as strong as it was for the people of Israel. He sent the great prophet Elijah to call them back, and He sent an even greater Prophet—His Son, Jesus—to save us from our sins and bring us back to Him.

LET'S PRAY: Lord God, You are an amazing God. Even when Your people turned away and a terrible king ruled over them, You sent them Your great prophet Elijah. Make my faith strong like Elijah's so I can boldly tell my family, friends, and neighbors how You sent Jesus, Your Son, to save us. Amen.

107

When Elijah Wanted to Quit

1 Kings 19; 2 Kings 2

Describe a time you were sad and wanted to give up.

When God sent fire down on Mount Carmel, Elijah thought the Israelites would believe again. And maybe King Ahab's wife, Jezebel, would believe too. But no, she was even more furious at Elijah and wanted to kill him. Elijah was sad and discouraged. He turned and ran away. He went out into the wilderness, sat under a tree, and prayed for God to let him die. Then, he fell asleep.

An angel woke him up and pointed to some food cooking nearby. He told Elijah to get up and eat. Elijah ate and then fell back asleep. Again, the angel woke him, and Elijah got up and ate. Strengthened by that food, Elijah traveled forty days to Horeb (Mount Sinai), the same place where God appeared to Moses in the burning bush and gave His Ten Commandments to Israel.

Elijah entered a cave and God asked him, "What are you doing here, Elijah?" Elijah complained about the Israelites. They had torn down God's altars, killed His prophets, and worshiped other gods. Elijah was the only prophet of God left—and they wanted to kill him too.

God told Elijah to go out and stand on the mountain because He was about to pass by. So Elijah walked out of the cave. First, a strong wind rushed by the mountain, tearing rocks apart—but God was not in the wind. Then came a mighty earthquake, shaking the ground—but God was not in the earthquake. Then, a fire raged, blazing on the mountain— but God was not in the fire either.

Then, Elijah heard a small, quiet voice. God gently asked Elijah why he was there, and Elijah again complained about Israel turning against God. The Lord told him to go back.

He would replace King Ahab and raise up a prophet named Elisha to work with him. Elijah found Elisha, put his cloak over Elisha's shoulders, and Elisha started working with him.

Then, God told Elijah it was time to come home to heaven. Elijah and Elisha reached the Jordan River, and Elijah struck the water with his rolled-up cloak. The water divided, and the two prophets crossed the river on dry ground. Elijah asked Elisha what he could do for him before he left. Elisha asked for a double share of the Holy Spirit. Elijah promised Elisha would receive it if he saw Elijah being taken up to heaven.

While they were talking, fiery chariots and horses appeared. While Elisha watched, Elijah climbed on a chariot and rode up into heaven by a whirlwind. On the way, Elijah's cloak fell from his shoulders. Elisha picked it up and struck the Jordan River with it. The waters divided, and he walked across on dry ground. God had sent another great prophet just like Elijah.

There are times when we get really frustrated and sad, when we want to give up because no matter how hard we try, it doesn't seem good enough. That is when we open the Bible to hear God speak to us in His small, soft voice of love and kindness.

LET'S PRAY: Lord God, thank You for strengthening and comforting Elijah when he was discouraged. Speak to me with Your gentle voice in the Bible, and give me strength and courage for Jesus' sake. Amen.

Naaman and Elisha 2 Kings 5

Describe a time you were really, really sick.

After God took Elijah up into heaven, Elisha took his place as the prophet to Israel, the ten tribes in the north. God worked many amazing miracles through him, even raising a dead boy to life again. Many people in Israel started talking about Elisha. One was a young girl whose name we don't even know.

When she was little, some soldiers from a country called Syria came in and attacked her town. They took her from her family and made her work in the house of Naaman (NAY-uh-muhn), an important leader in Syria's army. The little Israelite girl could have really hated Naaman and his people, but God helped her love them and serve them well—just like Joseph loved and served his masters in Egypt many, many years before.

One day, Naaman got leprosy, a terrible disease no doctor could cure. The Israelite girl told Naaman's wife she wished he would go see Elisha. She said confidently, "He would cure him of his leprosy." Naaman would do anything to be healed. He told his king what the little girl said, and his king wrote a letter to the king of Israel.

When the king of Israel read the letter, he got really upset. He didn't believe Elisha could heal lepers. He thought the king of Syria just wanted an excuse to come and attack Israel. But then Elisha sent a note to the king that said, "Let him come now to me, that he may know that there is a prophet in Israel."

So Naaman went to Elisha's house. He brought along great rewards if Elisha could heal him. But Elisha wouldn't even come to the door. Instead, Elisha's servant told Naaman to go and wash himself seven times in the Jordan River.

Naaman was furious. He expected the prophet to come down to meet him. He thought Elisha would stand and wave his hands over the diseased spot. He was so mad he was ready to ride back home. He told his servant every river in his country was better than the dirty old Jordan River.

But his servant reminded Naaman of how earlier he was ready to do anything to have his leprosy healed—no matter how hard it would be. Why not do the simple thing the prophet said and go wash himself in the Jordan River?

Naaman listened, went down, and washed himself in the Jordan seven times. When he came out, he was completely healed. He was so happy he rushed back to thank Elisha.

Many lepers came to Jesus too. Jesus loved them and healed each one. Jesus loves you too. He has that same power to cure you of every sickness you will ever get. And He promises that on the Last Day, He will come back and you will never get sick or hurt again.

LET'S PRAY: Lord God, thank You for healing Naaman and all those lepers during Jesus' life. Whenever I am sick or hurting, help my body to heal and give me patience to wait until I feel better. Remind me that when Jesus comes back, He will take away all sickness and disease forever. In Jesus' name I pray. Amen.

Jonah: The Prophet Who Said No

When was the last time your parents told you to do something you didn't want to do?

Prophets like Elijah and Elisha taught God's people how much He loved them and reminded them of the Savior He promised to send. But God also loved the people in other nations who did not know Him. One of those nations was called Assyria (uh-SEER-ee-uh).

The Assyrians were strong and mighty; they were very selfish and cruel. So, the Lord sent a prophet named Jonah (JOH-nuh) to warn them to stop doing bad things and ask God to forgive them. But Jonah hated the Assyrians. He was afraid God would change His mind, forgive them, and save them. So, Jonah got on a ship and started to sail as far away as he could go.

But God loved the Assyrians and wouldn't let Jonah sail away. He sent a great storm on the sea, big enough to scare even the sailors. They were all scared and prayed to their gods. But none of their gods were real, so the storm kept raging. Then, they found Jonah sleeping in the boat, so they woke him up and told him to pray too.

Jonah told them his God sent the storm because he was running away. They had to throw him into the water. The sailors asked God to forgive them and then threw Jonah into the sea. Right away, the winds stopped and the sea grew calm. The sailors worshiped God and thanked Him.

Down in the water, Jonah was sinking. He prayed, and God sent a huge fish to swallow him and save him. Jonah stayed inside that fish praying and thanking God for three days and three nights. Then, the fish swam up to shore and spit Jonah back out.

Again, God told Jonah to go to the city where the Assyrian king lived, a large city named Nineveh (NIN-uh-vuh). He had to warn them they would be destroyed in forty days if they didn't stop sinning and turn to God. This time Jonah went and did what God said. The people of Nineveh believed him. They put on really rough clothes, stopped eating, and begged God to save them. God felt sorry for them and decided not to destroy them.

But Jonah was not happy. He sat down in the desert outside of town hoping God would change His mind and go ahead and destroy Nineveh after forty days. God told Jonah He cared about all the people of Nineveh and didn't want any of them to die.

Jesus came to save all people of every nation by His life and His death on the cross. Now God sends you and me to tell everyone that God loves them and Jesus has saved them—even the bullies who make our lives hard.

LET'S PRAY: Lord God, thank You for loving the people of Nineveh and sending Jonah. Thank You for forgiving Jonah and giving him a second chance to obey You. Forgive me when I don't tell others about Your love and about Jesus like I should. Help me to love them like You do, and help me to want them to know how Jesus saved them. In Jesus' name. Amen.

The Northern Kingdom Ends

Name one of your mom or dad's rules that doesn't seem fair. Ask them to help you understand why they made that rule.

All of us have to follow rules, even your mom and dad. Sometimes it feels like rules are there only to take away our fun. Maybe you can't cross the street to play with your friends unless you stop and look both ways first to make sure no cars are coming. If you run across without looking, you won't be able to cross the street to play with those friends for a whole week!

Maybe that rule doesn't sound fair, but your mom and dad drive cars. They know when a child suddenly runs out from between parked cars, it is very hard to stop in time. Parents don't make up that rule because they want to take away your fun—they love you and don't want you to get hit by a car and hurt really badly.

God gives rules to protect us from things He knows will hurt us. One rule He made for His people of Israel was that they had to worship only Him. He made that rule because He is the only one who could save them from their sins and bring them to heaven to live with Him forever.

So God gave them the beautiful temple in Jerusalem and said they must go there three times each year. These would be happy times when they remembered all the good things He did for Israel and learned about His promise to send their Savior.

But the ten tribes in the north loved serving the false gods their neighbors served. They liked doing things that felt right—even when they hurt other people. The prophets warned them God would destroy their nation, but they loved doing wrong, and they refused to turn back. They kept on serving their false gods and treating people badly.

Finally, time ran out for the Northern Kingdom. The Lord raised up Assyria, the same country Jonah visited nearly seventy years before. It attacked Israel and captured all their cities one by one. The Assyrians killed many people and dragged away the ones who were left. The ten tribes were scattered; they disappeared, and they never came back together to form a nation again. Now only the kingdom of Judah was left in the south.

Ever since Adam and Eve disobeyed God and ate the fruit He told them not to eat, people have been breaking God's rules. We deserve for God to take us off His earth and drive us away from Him forever.

But our God loves us and is patient and kind. He wants all of us to come back to Him and live with Him forever. That is why He sent Jesus. Jesus kept all God's rules, and on the cross God punished Him for every time we break His rules. Now Jesus sends us to tell everyone just how much He loves them and how He died to save them from their sins too.

LET'S PRAY: Lord God, our heavenly Father, thank You for forgiving my sins for Jesus' sake. Give me courage to share Your story with all my family, friends, and neighbors, so they can also be forgiven and live with You in heaven forever. Amen.

Isaiah: Prophet to a Cold Nation

Which holiday do you like more: Christmas or Easter? Why?

The Northern Kingdom wandered so far from God that He brought in the Assyrians to punish the nation and carry it away. But what was happening in the Southern Kingdom of Judah?

They had the temple in Jerusalem. They had the priests and the Levites. King David's children were their kings. With all those good things, the people of Judah should have been making God happy, right?

Sadly, no. Judah was not much better than Israel. They did have some good kings who believed in God and tried to lead the people of Judah to serve Him. But there were also many bad kings who turned from God to worship things that weren't gods at all.

So what did God do when kings led His people away? He sent prophets to Judah just like He sent Elijah and Elisha to Israel. The first prophet we will look at is Isaiah (eye-ZAY-uh).

Isaiah talked a lot to Judah's kings. He told the bad kings they needed to ask God to forgive them, or God would destroy Jerusalem like He destroyed the Northern Kingdom. Isaiah also talked to the good kings who trusted God. He reminded them God would protect them, even when strong nations came near and scared them. His words made them brave to do what was right and serve God.

But the most important thing Isaiah did was to teach Judah and us about the Savior God had promised to Adam and Eve in the garden. Isaiah wrote these things about Jesus seven hundred years before He was even born!

Isaiah told us about Jesus' mother: "Behold, the virgin shall conceive and bear a son, and shall call His name Immanuel [which means 'God with us']" (Isaiah 7:14). Jesus' mother was the Virgin Mary.

Isaiah told us who the baby Jesus was: "For to us a child is born, to us a son is given; and the government shall be upon His shoulder, and His name shall be called Wonderful Counselor, Mighty God, Everlasting Father, Prince of Peace" (Isaiah 9:6).

Isaiah wrote about the Holy Spirit coming down upon Jesus after His Baptism: "Behold My servant, whom I uphold, My chosen, in whom My soul delights; I have put My Spirit upon Him; He will bring forth justice to the nations" (Isaiah 42:1).

Isaiah wrote about Jesus dying on the cross for us: "He was pierced for our transgressions; He was crushed for our iniquities; upon Him was the chastisement that brought us peace, and with His wounds we are healed" (Isaiah 53:5).

He wrote about Jesus being buried: "And they made His grave with the wicked and with a rich man in His death, although He had done no violence, and there was no deceit in His mouth" (Isaiah 53:9).

Finally, Isaiah even wrote about Jesus rising from the dead: "He shall see His offspring; He shall prolong His days; the will of the LORD shall prosper in His hand" (Isaiah 53:10).

Isaiah wrote about both Christmas and Easter. Both days are wonderful because they show us Jesus, our Savior.

LET'S PRAY: Lord God, our heavenly Father, thank You for showing us how Jesus would come and take away our sins forever. Help me to hear Isaiah's words and always believe in Jesus, my Savior. Amen.

King Hezekiah Prays

Describe a time you thought something really bad was about to happen.

The prophet Isaiah was sent to four different kings. One was a really bad king named Ahaz. He destroyed some of the pans and bowls in the temple, and he threw others away. He even shut the doors of the temple and made the priests stop holding services and offering sacrifices to God. He filled Jerusalem with altars to all kinds of false gods. God sent Isaiah to warn King Ahaz to turn away from his false gods and lead Judah back to their true God, but Ahaz refused to listen. After King Ahaz died, his son Hezekiah (hez-ih-KIGH-ah) became king.

Hezekiah was a good king who loved God very much. He was one of Judah's best kings, the best since King David. He trusted the Lord's promise to send the Savior, and he worked hard to lead Judah back to Him. He removed all his father's altars to false gods from Jerusalem. He opened the temple doors and told the priests to start having services and offering sacrifices again. He even had a great celebration of the Passover—the first great celebration since King David!

But Hezekiah was afraid. After the Assyrians destroyed Israel, they marched down into Judah. One by one, they captured every city, even those that had big, strong walls. Finally, there was only one city left. The Assyrians came up against Jerusalem and formed a big circle all around it with their huge army.

Hezekiah looked out on that army, and he knew his army was much too small to push them away. His walls were strong but not strong enough to keep the Assyrians out.

The Assyrian king sent a messenger to King Hezekiah and all his people. He shouted that Hezekiah should not trust God. He told the people of Judah to open the city gates and come out to him. He claimed that Assyria's gods were much stronger than Judah's God. The king of Assyria wrote a letter in which he made fun of God. His messengers carried the letter to King Hezekiah.

Hezekiah took that letter to the temple. He rolled it out before God and prayed for God to listen and read how the Assyrian king was making fun of Him. God sent Isaiah to Hezekiah to promise that God would drag the Assyrian army back to Assyria without letting them hurt Jerusalem.

That night, God sent an angel who went through the Assyrian camp killing many, many soldiers. The next morning, the Assyrians saw all the dead bodies and ran away back to Assyria.

God created many, many angels. He sends them to guard us and protect us. We don't ever need to be afraid of what other people want to do to us—or even what the devil wants to do to us. God is so much stronger, and Jesus died and rose again to save us. We are always safe in His hands.

LET'S PRAY: Lord God, our Father, thank You for listening to the prayer of King Hezekiah and for sending an angel to protect Jerusalem. Help me be confident that You will never forget me or take away Your guardian angels. I pray in Jesus' name. Amen.

Judah Goes into Exile

Have you ever done something bad and gotten in big trouble because of it? What happened? Ask your mom or dad if they have ever gotten into big trouble.

Judah lasted longer than the kingdom of Israel in the north. It also had good kings like Hezekiah who believed God's warnings and His promise of forgiveness through Jesus. These good kings helped lead the people of Judah to praise and serve God instead of the false gods of the nations around them.

But Judah had many bad kings too. The worst of them all was Hezekiah's own son, Manasseh (muh-NAS-uh). He closed the doors of the temple and stopped the services and sacrifices again. He also taught the people to worship and serve false gods, killed many people, and did many other horrible things. He led his people so far from God that the Lord decided He would destroy Judah like He had destroyed Israel. Manasseh was followed by another bad king, his son Amon (AY-mun).

But there was one more good king for Judah: Amon's son Josiah. Josiah was only eight years old when he became king! Josiah loved God and wanted to serve Him alone. He repaired and cleaned out the temple and started the sacrifices again, and he went all through the land tearing down all the altars to false gods. He even went into the land of Israel, the Northern Kingdom, and destroyed the two golden calves that Israel's first king, Jeroboam, had built.

But it was too late for Judah. One day Josiah died in battle, and one by one his three sons and one grandson became king after him. All of them turned the people of Judah away from God. So God brought in another mighty kingdom: Babylon. The Babylonians captured Jerusalem and took the next generation of leaders far away into the land of Babylon. They left the temple and the city walls standing and let the poorest people stay behind to live in Jerusalem.

But even these poor people rose up against God. They disobeyed the king of Babylon, so he came back a second time and captured Jerusalem. This time, he burned the city with fire, tore down its mighty walls, and destroyed Solomon's temple. Almost all the people who were left were taken to live in Babylon, far away. There they would wait seventy years until God was ready to bring them back home again.

Sometimes we make bad decisions like the kings and people of Judah did. We turn our back on God and do all kinds of bad things that hurt other people and even ourselves. But just as God watched over His people who were living in Babylon, God will watch over you. He is always ready to forgive you, wash away your sins for Jesus' sake, and bring you home to heaven when Jesus returns. As long as you are still alive, it is not too late to ask God to forgive you again.

LET'S PRAY: Heavenly Father, thank You that it is not too late for me to see when I have done wrong and come back to ask You to forgive me for Jesus' sake. Help me be like King Josiah, telling other people about Your love. I pray in Jesus' name. Amen.

Jeremiah: Dedicated to God's People

Book of Jeremiah

Have you ever tried to convince a friend to stop doing something wrong? Why might that be hard?

Just like the Northern Kingdom, Judah in the south disobeyed God, so He brought in the Babylonians to destroy Jerusalem. But even before the Babylonians came, God loved His people and sent a prophet to warn them. Jeremiah (jer-uh-MY-uh) warned King Josiah's sons to turn around and come back to God. But the kings and the people wouldn't listen—instead, they tried to make Jeremiah stop talking to them.

Once, the people put ropes around Jeremiah and lowered him down into a cistern, a tank that collected rainwater. There was no water in the cistern, just deep mud. They wanted to leave him there to die, but a brave servant convinced the king to send a group of soldiers to pull Jeremiah out with ropes.

But even worse, false prophets came and told the people that Jeremiah was lying. They told the kings and the people everything was okay. The city would enjoy peace, not the war Jeremiah kept talking about.

God told Jeremiah to write a long scroll of His warnings and promises to King Jehoiakim of Judah. While the scroll was being read, the king took a knife, cut off the part already read to him, and tossed it into his fire. Because the king treated God's words so badly, God told the king Jerusalem would be captured and he would have no children to sit on the throne of David.

After King Jehoiakim died, his son Jehoiachin became king. Three months later, the king of Babylon captured him and took him to Babylon. His uncle Zedekiah was made the next king.

When King Zedekiah later disobeyed the king of Babylon, Nebuchadnezzar came back and destroyed Jerusalem and the temple. Jeremiah wrote a very sad Bible book called Lamentations. It reminds us of how badly the people of Judah suffered for their sins. It also lets us see how much Jesus would suffer when He died for us on the cross.

The king of Babylon left some very, very poor people behind, and Jeremiah decided to stay with them to share God's words of love and of warning. But even these people refused to listen; they ran away from the king of Babylon and forced Jeremiah to go with them to Egypt. But Jeremiah warned them the king of Babylon would find them there. You can't get away from God.

Sometimes we aren't a lot different from the people of Jerusalem. We know what God wants us to do, but we want to do things our way, not His. Even though God's Word warns us that bad things happen when we turn away from God, we keep going and turning away from God. But God still loves us. He speaks to us through Jeremiah's words today, making us feel bad about what we have done and showing us how He gave His only Son, Jesus, to die on the cross to save us from our sins.

LET'S PRAY: Lord God, Your patience and love are truly amazing. Over and over, Your people disobeyed You, but You still loved them and watched over them. We are no different from them, turning from You again and again. Thank You for loving us still and calling us back to You for Jesus' sake. Amen.

Ezekiel: Prophet in Exile

Have you ever wondered if God is too far away to hear you?

Jerusalem had been captured for the first time. The Babylonian king Nebuchadnezzar (neb-uh-kuhd-NEH-zer) had carried away most of the people who were leaders or who had skills building or working with wood, stone, and metal. He left the poorest people behind, and Jeremiah stayed with them. The temple was still standing in Jerusalem, but what happened to the Jews who were taken far away to Babylon? Did God forget all about them? Did He hear their prayers?

Yes, God cared about His people who were in Babylon. In fact, He raised up two great prophets out of that first group of exiles. One was named Daniel, and the other was Ezekiel (ih-ZEE-kee-uhl). God worked through both of these men to speak to the Jews in exile and to protect them.

Ezekiel was not only a prophet, but he was also a priest. That was important because the Jews living in Babylon believed the lies the false prophets kept telling them. These prophets said they would all be going home soon because the temple was still standing in Jerusalem. Jeremiah even had to write a letter from Jerusalem to tell them they should build houses and plant vineyards because they would be in Babylon a long, long time before God would bring them back home.

God gave Ezekiel a vision. He saw Solomon's temple in Jerusalem. When Solomon brought the ark of the covenant into this temple, suddenly the cloud of God's glory appeared and went into the temple, just as Moses watched it enter the tabernacle on Mount Sinai long before. But then Ezekiel saw the bright cloud of God's glory leaving the temple and going outside the city of Jerusalem.

Ezekiel told the people the temple would be destroyed, the walls would be torn down, and the houses and buildings in the city would be burned down to the ground because the people had turned away from God. The king and many other Jews would be taken away from Jerusalem just as they had been.

The people didn't believe Ezekiel until they heard the news that Jerusalem had been captured again, and this time the temple had been completely destroyed. The exiles felt that God was against them and they would never go home. So, Ezekiel started telling them that God was with them. He would watch over them and protect them. He would come as their Good Shepherd and gather them together. And when seventy years were over, a new king would let the Jews go home and rebuild Jerusalem and the temple.

Finally, the Lord showed Ezekiel a new temple, which would be greater than the old temple. God's glory would come to His people, and He would build an everlasting kingdom for them—and never take His glory away from them again. That was Jesus and His glorious kingdom, which He gives to every person who believes and trusts in Him.

LET'S PRAY: Lord God, forgive me for leaving You so often. Forgive me for Jesus' sake and remain in my heart always, that I may tell others about Your love and live in Your glorious presence forever. In Jesus' name. Amen.

The Fiery Furnace Daniel 3

Have you ever had to do something really scary that might get you hurt?

Ezekiel was one of the two great prophets God raised up from the first group of exiles to Babylon. The other was Daniel and his three friends Hananiah (han-uh-NIGH-uh), Mishael (MISH-ay-el), and Azariah (az-uh-RYE-uh). You might know them better by the new names they got in Babylon: Shadrach (SHAD-rak), Meshach (MEE-shak), and Abednego (uh-BED-nih-goh). And the king called Daniel a new name too: Belteshazzar (bel-tih-SHAY-zur).

These four friends were young when they were taken into exile. They were trained to serve as wise men in Nebuchadnezzar's court. God worked through Daniel and his friends to make sure Nebuchadnezzar and the other kings who followed him would know and honor Israel's God and protect His people.

But Nebuchadnezzar was a proud man. He built a huge golden statue of himself that rose high above the ground. Nebuchadnezzar ordered all the people to bow down to his statue when they heard the music start. Anyone who would not bow down would be thrown into a fiery furnace.

But Daniel's three friends were not afraid of the king. They knew God was the only one who ruled over heaven and earth, and they refused to bow down to the king's statue. Nebuchadnezzar was furious. He repeated his directions and told them if they did not obey, they would be thrown into the furnace, and no god would be able to deliver them out of his hands.

Shadrach, Meshach, and Abednego told the king, "Our God whom we serve is able to deliver us from the burning fiery furnace, and He will deliver us out of your hand, O king. But if not, be it known to you, O king, that we will not serve your gods or worship the golden image that you have set up."

Nebuchadnezzar was so furious, he told his servants to heat up the furnace even hotter. He ordered his strongest, bravest soldiers to tie up the three men and throw them into the fiery furnace. The furnace was so hot that when the soldiers pushed them in, the flames leaped out and killed the soldiers. But when the king looked into the fiery furnace, he was astonished. He didn't see just three men: "I see four men unbound, walking in the midst of the fire, and they are not hurt; and the appearance of the fourth is like a son of the gods."

He was so astonished he told the three servants of God to come out. When they came out, everyone rushed up to see if they were burned—but they were totally unhurt. Their hair was not singed, and their clothes did not even smell like smoke. Nebuchadnezzar passed a law that no one should say anything against the God of Shadrach, Meshach, and Abednego—because he said "no other god is able to rescue in this way."

God had shown Nebuchadnezzar that He is mighty, and He made sure that Daniel's three friends could remind the king to take good care of the Jews.

LET'S PRAY: Lord God, thank You for protecting Shadrach, Meshach, and Abednego and for giving them such strong faith in You. Give me that strong faith too, for Jesus' sake. Amen.

Daniel in the Lions' Den

Daniel 6

Has someone ever tried really hard to get you in trouble?

Daniel was very wise and successful. God gave him great wisdom and the ability to understand special dreams that the kings of Babylon had, much like Joseph did in Egypt. Finally, after seventy years, God raised up two nations, the Medes and the Persians, to join together to capture the kingdom of Babylon.

One of the new kings was named Darius the Mede. King Darius liked Daniel. In fact, King Darius was so pleased with Daniel that he made him ruler over one third of his kingdom. Since Daniel did so well with that third of the kingdom, Darius decided to make him ruler over all the land.

That did not make the other officials very happy. They wanted Daniel's power and glory. So they looked closely, but Daniel was so honest, hardworking, and truthful. They could not find a single bad thing he had done. So they decided to make something up.

They told Darius he should command all the people in his kingdom to pray to no god but him for a whole month. And if anyone prayed to a different god, they would be thrown into a den or pit full of hungry lions. Darius was very pleased with their idea, so he made their suggestion the law of the land.

Daniel read the new law but trusted God to protect him. He kept kneeling down in his house and praying to God just the way he had done for all those years. But one day, the jealous leaders came through the door and caught him while he was praying.

They rushed him to King Darius and told him that Daniel had broken his law and had to be thrown into the lions' den. The king was very sorry and looked all day for some way to save Daniel, but his foolish law made it impossible.

Sadly, he ordered his soldiers to put Daniel into the lions' den. But as they were putting him in, the king said, "May your God, whom you serve continually, deliver you!" A large stone was brought and laid at the door to the cave or den, and it was sealed.

All that night, the king couldn't sleep. Early the next morning, he rose and hurried to the den of lions. In a sad voice, he called, "O Daniel, servant of the living God, has your God, whom you serve continually, been able to deliver you from the lions?" And he listened closely.

Suddenly, a voice from behind the rock called, "O king, my God has sent His angel and shut the lions' mouths, and they have not harmed me."

The king was so very happy! He ordered Daniel to be released from the lions' den, and then he commanded his soldiers to throw those wicked rulers who had accused Daniel into the lions' den. And before they reached the bottom, the lions killed them all.

LET'S PRAY: Lord God, You created the lions and every one of us. Thank You for closing the mouths of the lions to protect Daniel. Teach me to trust You to protect me from all harm and danger. I pray in Jesus' name. Amen.

Esther Saves Israel Book of Esther

Have you ever wanted to help someone but were afraid you would get in trouble if you tried?

When Judah was taken to Babylon, it was a dangerous time for God's people. But the Lord raised up leaders like Daniel to protect them. This time we will see God raise up a young Jewish girl named Esther to save His people. Esther lost both her mother and father when she was young, so she was raised by her cousin Mordecai (MAWR-dih-kigh).

At that time, the king over the Medes and Persians was named Ahasuerus (ah-has-oo-AY-rus). One night he got mad at his queen and divorced her. When he wanted a new queen, he gathered many beautiful young women together. When the king met Esther, he chose her to be his new queen.

One of the king's officials was a very evil, selfish man named Haman (HAY-muhn). The king made him very powerful in his kingdom and commanded all the people to bow down whenever Haman passed by—but Mordecai refused. That made Haman so angry he decided not just to ask the king to kill Mordecai, but to kill all the Jews. The king told him to write a law and choose the day he wanted the Jews to be killed.

Mordecai told Esther about the new law. He wanted her to go to her king and beg him to save the Jews. But Esther was afraid to go in. Anyone who went to talk to the king without being invited would be killed, and the king had not asked to see Esther in a whole month.

Mordecai told Esther she was not safe just because she was queen. So Esther prayed for three days and nights, and then she went in to talk to the king without being asked. He was pleased to see her and forgave her for breaking the rule. Then, he promised to give her anything she asked for. She asked him to come to a banquet in his honor and to invite Haman.

Haman was really happy, thinking the queen really liked him.

The next night, the king and Haman came to her banquet. Then after supper, the king asked Esther what she wanted. She said someone was trying to kill her and all her people. He became angry and asked who dared to kill his queen and her people. She said it was Haman.

The king was furious and stomped out into the garden. When he left, Haman ran to Esther and begged her to save his life. Just as the king returned, he saw Haman falling on Esther. The king thought he was attacking her—so he ordered Haman to be taken out and killed.

The king gave Mordecai the place that Haman had and told him to let the Jews defend themselves on the day Haman had planned to kill them.

LET'S PRAY: Lord God, many times Your people were in great danger, but You defended them and protected them with people like Esther. Thank You for sending Your Son, Jesus, to protect me from all danger—especially the danger of hell. Give me faith and joy to share that great news with others. In Jesus' name. Amen.

131

Rebuilding Jerusalem and the Temple

Books of Ezra and Nehemiah

Ask your parents who built your church and what it was like back then. If they don't know, ask your pastor.

The people of Judah lived in Babylon for seventy years. God led them with prophets like Jeremiah and Ezekiel, and He protected them with people like Daniel and Esther. But the time came for them to return and rebuild the city of Jerusalem and the temple of their God.

God led King Cyrus to let the people of Judah return home. He gave the priests and leaders many things Nebuchadnezzar had taken out of Solomon's old temple. The Jews would use these items in the new temple.

But rebuilding the temple wasn't easy. Many neighbors didn't want Jerusalem to be rebuilt. One of these neighbors was the Samaritans (suh-MAIR-ih-tuhns). At first, they wanted to help rebuild the temple, but the Jews wouldn't let them because they were not true Israelites. That made the Samaritans angry enough to try to stop the Jews from rebuilding the temple. But prophets like Zechariah (zek-uh-RYE-uh) and Haggai (HAG-eye) encouraged them until the temple was completed.

Some of the older Jews had been children when Nebuchadnezzar took them from Jerusalem. They still remembered Solomon's beautiful old temple—and they thought this one looked so plain. The prophet Haggai asked, "Who is left among you who saw this house in its former glory? How do you see it now? Is it not as nothing in your eyes? . . . I will fill this house with glory, says the LORD of hosts. . . . The latter glory of this house shall be greater than the former" (Haggai 2:3, 7, 9).

The glory that would fill this temple would not be gold and silver like Solomon used to build his temple. It would be God's promised Savior, His own Son, Jesus Christ, who would stand in the courts of this temple and teach the Jews all about God His Father.

Fifty-eight years after the temple was finished, a priest named Ezra came back to Jerusalem. He restored the worship services at the temple and encouraged the Jews to serve God and bring Him their offerings and sacrifices.

Thirteen years after that, a Jew named Nehemiah (nee-huh-MY-uh) learned Jerusalem was still in bad shape. The walls were still piles of rubble, and enemies were making life hard for the Jews living there. So the king gave Nehemiah permission to return to Jerusalem and rebuild the city walls. Judah was back up on its feet again.

Over four hundred years would go by before the New Testament began and Jesus came as God had promised to Adam and Eve and to so many others. The world changed a lot in that time too. The Medes and Persians lost the land of Canaan to the Macedonians. After a few hundred years, the Macedonians lost it to the Romans.

But this new temple would still be standing in Jerusalem, waiting for God's promised Son, our Savior, to be born and to come and teach in its courts.

LET'S PRAY: Heavenly Father, thank You for raising up brave men and women to rebuild the temple so it would be ready for our Lord Jesus to come. Make my heart ready for Him to come and be my Lord, even as He died on the cross to be my Savior. In Jesus' name. Amen.

The

NEW TESTAMENT

The Birth of John the Baptist Foretold

Luke 1:5–25

Have you ever prayed and asked God to do something for you but then given up when nothing happened?

When it was almost the time God wanted to send His Son into the world, He sent an angel named Gabriel (GAY-bree-uhl) to the temple in Jerusalem. Gabriel appeared to a priest who was burning incense in the Holy Place, the front room of the temple. The priest's name was Zechariah (zek-uh-RYE-uh). Zechariah and his wife, Elizabeth, both loved God and trusted His promise to send the Savior. Many years before, Zechariah had prayed that God would give them a child, but now they were very old, and no child had ever come.

When Gabriel suddenly appeared, Zechariah was terrified. The angel told him, "Do not be afraid, Zechariah, for your prayer has been heard, and your wife Elizabeth will bear you a son, and you shall call his name John."

The angel told him that his son would be great, and he would go before the Lord as His mighty messenger. He would prepare God's people to receive His Son, whom He had promised so long ago to Adam and Eve in the Garden of Eden after they had eaten the forbidden fruit.

This great promise surprised Zechariah very much. He answered, "How shall I know this? For I am an old man, and my wife is advanced in years." He didn't believe God's promise because he thought Elizabeth was way too old to have a baby.

The angel answered, "I am Gabriel. I stand in the presence of God, and I was sent to speak to you and to bring you this good news. And behold, you will be silent and unable to speak until the day that these things take place, because you did not believe my words, which will be fulfilled in their time." Sure enough, when the angel left him, Zechariah came out of the temple but couldn't say a word.

When his time to serve at the temple ended, he returned home and Elizabeth became pregnant, and the baby started growing inside her.

Sometimes, we pray for things, as Zechariah did, and it seems like God doesn't hear—or He doesn't care. But God hears all our prayers, and He promises to answer all of them. Sometimes, He gives us the things we ask for because those are best for us. Sometimes, He says no because He wants to give us something better than we could ever think of. Sometimes, He wants us to wait—like Zechariah— because His time has not come yet.

But whatever His answer might be, you can be sure it will be the very best for you.

Gabriel Visits Mary

When you look at a manger scene at Christmastime, what do you think about little baby Jesus?

Six months after Zechariah's wife, Elizabeth, became pregnant, God sent the angel Gabriel to a northern town called Nazareth to a young woman named Mary. She was betrothed to a man named Joseph. They had promised to marry each other and were waiting for their wedding, when they could move in together and start their family.

The angel appeared to Mary and said, "Greetings, O favored one, the Lord is with you!" Mary wasn't expecting an angel to come to her, and she was shaken up. She thought carefully about what he had said, and she wondered what he meant. She wondered what he was going to say to her next— would it be bad news or good news?

Gabriel said, "Do not be afraid, Mary, for you have found favor with God. And behold, you will bear a son, and you shall call His name Jesus." He told her this child would be great and would be called "the Son of the Most High."

Mary believed the angel, but she wondered how she would become the mother of this child. She wasn't married to Joseph yet.

The angel told her the Holy Spirit would come to her and use His mighty power to give her this baby. He added, "Therefore the child to be born will be called holy—the Son of God."

The angel said Jesus would be great; He would rule on the throne of His father David and reign over the house of Jacob forever. Mary knew this was the Savior God promised so long ago to Adam and Eve; to Abraham, Isaac, and Jacob; and to King David. Since He is God's own Son, His kingdom will never end.

Finally, the angel Gabriel told Mary that her relative Elizabeth was pregnant because of God's great power, even though she was way too old to have a baby.

Mary believed the angel. She was ready to offer herself to be part of God's loving plan. She replied, "I am the servant of the Lord; let it be to me according to your word."

It's neat that Jesus had a human mother just like you and me and every other boy and girl. Since Jesus lived as a boy on this earth, He knows what it is like to be a child, then grow up to be an adult, as you will one day. And since Jesus is a human, He was able to take our sins from us, carry them to the cross, and suffer and die there in our place.

But it's even better that Jesus' Father was God Almighty, and not a human birth father like our dads. That means Jesus doesn't have our sinful nature—He is holy and perfect.

That means Jesus was able to keep all God's Commandments in our place and earn our place in heaven. And since He is God, Jesus was able to destroy the devil, death, and hell for us.

LET'S PRAY: Lord God, heavenly Father, thank You for the wonderful words the angel Gabriel brought to Mary. Thank You for sending Your only Son to be her Son, our strong Brother who saved us from our sins. In Jesus' name. Amen.

Mary Visits Elizabeth

Luke 1:39–56

Do you ever wish you could trade places with boys or girls who are more popular or have families with lots of money and things?

The angel Gabriel told Mary that God had chosen her to be the mother of His own Son. He also told her how God had used His great power to give a baby to her elderly relative Elizabeth. After the angel left, Mary decided to leave Nazareth and go visit Zechariah and Elizabeth in Judah (JOO-duh).

She traveled quickly and came to Zechariah's house. When she saw Elizabeth, Mary said hello. Right at that moment, Elizabeth's baby started leaping inside her. She was filled with the Holy Spirit and told Mary, "Blessed are you among women, and blessed is the fruit of your womb! And why is this granted to me that the mother of my Lord should come to me?" Yes, even though Mary hadn't said a word about being pregnant, Elizabeth knew she was carrying a baby, and she knew this baby was the Lord, the promised Son of God.

Mary was amazed God had chosen her to be the mother of His precious Son. Mary was not famous; her family wasn't powerful; they didn't have a lot of money. Yet God chose her. He passed by all the rich, powerful, and famous families, and chose Mary of Nazareth to be the mother of His Son. She began praising Him in words we call "The Song of Mary": "My soul magnifies the Lord, and my spirit rejoices in God my Savior." The more Mary thought about it, the more she realized how amazing God is. "He who is mighty has done great things for me, and holy is His name." And she praised God for keeping His promise to Abraham, Isaac, and Jacob: "He has helped His servant Israel, in remembrance of His mercy, as He spoke to our fathers, to Abraham and to his offspring forever."

Mary spent three months with Zechariah and Elizabeth. These must have been wonderful days, talking about God's great love and feeling the babies grow inside them.

God didn't choose Mary and Elizabeth because they had a lot of friends or nice big homes or a bunch of money. He chose them because He loved them. God chose you for the same reason. It doesn't matter to Him if everyone at school knows you or not or likes you or not. It doesn't matter if your family has a lot of money or none at all. God gave His own Son, Jesus, to save you, and He made you His own child in Baptism. Now, He wants to work through you to make other boys and girls His own sons and daughters through faith in Jesus.

LET'S PRAY: Lord God, heavenly Father, thank You for choosing me to be Your child and for saving me through Your Son, Jesus. Give me Your Holy Spirit, that I may be brave and filled with love and joy to tell other people about Jesus' great love. In Jesus' name. Amen.

The Birth of John the Baptist

Did you ever have to keep a secret from someone and it was almost impossible to do so?

Mary stayed with Zechariah and Elizabeth until the time came for John the Baptist to be born. Then Mary returned home to Nazareth. When Elizabeth had her baby, all their neighbors celebrated with them and praised God for being so good and kind to them.

All this time, Zechariah remained silent, unable to speak—but surely he watched and listened and had so much he wanted to say! All through the nearly three months Mary had stayed with them, he couldn't say a word. And even after his baby was born, he still couldn't talk.

One more week went by, and Zechariah's son turned eight days old. For Israelite boys, this eighth day was very special. This was the day they were circumcised and given their very own names. Zechariah and Elizabeth's neighbors and relatives gathered to celebrate.

When it was time to name the baby, the guests wanted to name him Zechariah, after his father. But Elizabeth said, "No; he shall be called John." The neighbors and relatives were puzzled: "None of your relatives is called by this name." They turned to Zechariah to see what he wanted to name him. Zechariah took a writing tablet and wrote down in front of them all, "His name is John."

Suddenly, God opened Zechariah's mouth so he could talk again. Now at last, after holding all his thoughts inside for almost a year, Zechariah was able to praise and thank God the way he should have done when the angel Gabriel first spoke to him.

Zechariah was filled with the Holy Spirit and said some wonderful words we call the "Song of Zechariah." We call it a song because sometimes we sing it in church. In his song, he praised God for sending His Son to be our Savior, and he rejoiced that the promised Savior had come. He didn't say it in his song, but he knew that wonderful baby had been right there in his house, growing inside the Virgin Mary.

Then Zechariah looked at his own little baby. He told John, "And you, child, will be called the prophet of the Most High; for you will go before the Lord to prepare His ways." When John grew up, he did go before the Christ and made people ready to hear their Savior's wonderful words. Zechariah closed his song by speaking again about Mary's baby and the wonderful peace and eternal life He would win for all of us.

Keeping secrets is hard—especially when we have great good news to tell people. But the greatest, most happy news of all is something we never have to keep secret from our family, friends, and people at school and everywhere: God loves them and sent His Son to save them.

LET'S PRAY: Lord God, heavenly Father, thank You for bringing Zechariah to bold faith and confidence in Your promises, and for restoring his voice to tell all his relatives and neighbors that Your Son was coming at last. Give me confidence to tell everyone I know about how You sent Your Son as our Savior, so they, too, may know all about Jesus. In Jesus' name. Amen.

An Angel Visits Joseph

Matthew 1:18–25

Do you know children who live without their father or mother? What do you think is the worst part of that?

The time came for God to keep His promise to send the Savior. By the power of the Holy Spirit, His Son became a human baby, growing inside His mother, the Virgin Mary. When Joseph learned she was going to have a baby, that made him sad. He wanted Mary to be his wife and live with him in their home. He wanted to have babies together and raise their own family.

Joseph loved Mary very much and was worried about what would happen to her if he left her and made her raise her baby by herself. But for Joseph, it was even more important to do what God wanted. One of God's Ten Commandments says, "You shall not commit adultery." That means God wants babies to come from a mother and a father who are already married to each other.

As Joseph thought and prayed about it, he was afraid God would be upset with him if he married her. So Joseph decided to divorce Mary. But he would do it quietly, not telling anyone why he was ending their marriage. That would protect Mary from people who might want to hurt her.

After he made up his mind, Joseph fell asleep. But in his dreams, an angel told him not to be afraid to take Mary as his wife. The baby growing inside her was God's Son. The Lord wanted Joseph to give Mary's baby the name *Jesus* and raise Him as if He were his own son. The name *Jesus* means "the Lord saves." It was the perfect name for this baby, because He was the promised Savior, the Son of God, who saved us from our sins.

Joseph woke up from his dream and did everything the Lord told him to do. He took Mary as his wife. So when baby Jesus was born, Joseph was there to take care of Him like a father.

God loves you very much too, just like He loved His own Son, Jesus, and Joseph and Mary. If your mom and dad are living together with you, thank God for keeping them together. If they aren't together anymore and you are growing up with one but not the other, or if you aren't living with either your mother or your father, that is hard.

But remember that God will never forget you. He loves you and will always be by your side. He will give you everything you need and will wash away all your sins for Jesus' sake. And one more thing: Even if you don't have your mother or father with you anymore, God has made you His very own son or daughter for Jesus' sake. He is your heavenly Father, who will never grow old, get sick, or die. He'll never get tired of taking care of you and leave. He is in heaven right now preparing your forever home.

LET'S PRAY: Lord God, heavenly Father, thank You for making sure Joseph was there to be a father to Jesus, even though he wasn't Jesus' birth father. Thank You for choosing me as Your own child for Jesus' sake when You baptized me. Help me to serve You well and show the world what a great God and Savior I have. In Jesus' name. Amen.

The Birth of Jesus

What are some things you do to celebrate Jesus' birth at Christmas?

The time was coming for Mary to have her baby. Since this was God's own Son, you might expect Him to have been born in a big, shiny palace near the temple in the big city of Jerusalem. But God had very different plans.

Joseph and Mary were living and working in Nazareth, far to the north, when suddenly a command came from the emperor of Rome, Caesar Augustus. Luke wrote, "In those days a decree went out from Caesar Augustus that all the world should be registered. . . . And all went to be registered, each to his own town" (Luke 2:1, 3).

Caesar wanted to count how many people were in his empire. So Joseph had to go to his family's home town. It wasn't Jerusalem; it was the little town of Bethlehem (BETH-leh-hem), the home of his ancestor David.

But that was exactly what God had said would happen. Through the prophet Micah, God promised, "But you, O Bethlehem Ephrathah, who are too little to be among the clans of Judah, from you shall come forth for Me one who is to be ruler in Israel, whose coming forth is from of old, from ancient days" (Micah 5:2). God used a command from the Roman emperor to make the prophecy of Micah come true. Before the world was created, the Son of God came forth from His Father. And here in the little town of Bethlehem, He would be born to be ruler in Israel.

So Joseph and Mary left Nazareth and made their way to Bethlehem. By the time they arrived, the little town was full of Jewish descendants of David who had come to town to be counted. Joseph looked around for a place where he and Mary could stay, but it was a small town and he couldn't find any good place for Mary to have her baby. Every guest room was full.

Since he couldn't find a place inside a house or building, Joseph was forced to take Mary into a cave or stable where work animals like donkeys and oxen were kept out of the wind and rain. He cleared a little spot between the animals and made a bed for Mary. That's where Mary had her baby, God's own Son. She wrapped Him tightly in swaddling cloths, and since she didn't have a crib, she laid Him in a manger, the trough that held the animals' food.

That is hardly where we would expect to find God's newly born Son. He is so great and wonderful, He should have been lying in a soft, beautiful crib in a huge, warm palace. But the Son of God lay in straw, surrounded by the animals He created. He didn't come to be served by people but to serve them. God kept His promises to Adam and Eve; Abraham, Isaac, and Jacob; and King David. Their Descendant—the promised Savior—was born. He was finally here.

LET'S PRAY: Lord God, thank You for keeping Your promise to send Your Son to save us. Each Christmas, help me remember that His coming is the reason Christmas is so special. In Jesus' name. Amen.

The Angels and the Shepherds

What is your favorite present that you ever got for Christmas?

When Jesus was born, Mary wrapped Him in strips of cloth and laid Him in a manger, a feeding trough for animals.

In the fields outside of Bethlehem, shepherds were watching their sheep in the night. Suddenly, an angel appeared to them. He was shining in glory, and the even brighter glory of God was shining around them. This filled the shepherds with fear. The bright light and the shining angel reminded them of their sins and how they deserved to be punished by God.

But the angel told them, "Fear not, for behold, I bring you good news of great joy that will be for all the people. For unto you is born this day in the city of David a Savior, who is Christ the Lord." This was the promise God had given to Adam and Eve in the Garden of Eden and to so many others throughout the Old Testament.

What an amazing moment for the shepherds! The long-promised Savior had finally come—and He was somewhere over there in the little town of Bethlehem. The angel told them, "You will find a baby wrapped in swaddling cloths and lying in a manger." When they went searching through the town, they would be sure they had found the right baby.

When the angel finished, suddenly the sky was filled with angels who praised God and said, "Glory be to God on high, and on the earth, peace among those with whom He is pleased." God is pleased with us when we turn from our sins and trust His promise to forgive us for Jesus' sake. When our sins are forgiven, we have peace with God.

When the angels returned to heaven, the shepherds left their sheep and rushed off at once into Bethlehem to find the baby. When they found Him, they told Mary and Joseph what the angel had said to them. Mary listened closely and thought about what God was teaching her about her Son, our amazing Savior.

Then the shepherds went back to the fields. But they didn't keep the great news to themselves. The angel had said his good news was for *all* the people—and it would bring great joy to all who heard and believed God's promise to save them. The shepherds told people about the wonderful things God had done, and they praised Him for keeping His promise and sending His Son.

There are many things about Christmas that are really exciting. Certainly, the presents are part of that. You may get something so great you can't wait to tell your friends all about it. That is how the shepherds felt about the good news they had heard. The Savior of all people was born, and they had seen Him with their own eyes! They couldn't keep the good news to themselves. That same excitement makes it hard to keep the joy of Jesus' birth to ourselves.

LET'S PRAY: Heavenly Father, You sent an angel to tell the shepherds the good news of Jesus' birth. Like the shepherds, help me understand how great Jesus really is so that I trust Him as my Savior and am excited to tell the Good News to everyone I meet. In Jesus' name. Amen.

The Presentation of Jesus

Luke 2:22–38

What do you think it would have been like to hold baby Jesus and know you were holding God's Son?

When Jesus was forty days old, Joseph and Mary took Him to Jerusalem. Moses' Law required each firstborn boy to be presented to the Lord at the temple when he was forty days old. That very day, Joseph and Mary brought God's own Son to the temple to be presented to God His Father.

While they were there, Mary and Joseph met two older Jews. The first was a man named Simeon. Simeon loved God and was waiting for Him to send the Messiah. The Holy Spirit had revealed to him that he would see the Christ before he died. At this very time, the Holy Spirit led him to the temple and revealed to him that this baby Jesus was that promised Savior. Simeon took Jesus in his arms and said, "Lord, now You are letting Your servant go in peace, because my own eyes have seen Your salvation, which You have prepared before the face of all people."

We call this the "Song of Simeon." Sometimes, we sing it in church after we receive Holy Communion. We can go from the altar at peace and forgiven by God because our eyes have seen the body and blood of our Lord and Savior in the bread and wine. We remember Jesus died on the cross to save us from our sin.

When Simeon finished these words, he turned to Mary and told her that not everyone was going to be happy that Jesus was born. Some would reject Him and refuse to believe in Him. And Mary would feel great sorrow, like a sword piercing through her soul. Simeon was talking about the day when Mary would stand under Jesus' cross and watch Him die for her sins and ours.

There at the temple along with Simeon was an old, old woman named Anna. Her husband had died long ago when she was still a young woman. Now, she never left the temple but worshiped God and prayed night and day. After she saw Jesus, she spoke about Him to everyone who was waiting for the Messiah.

Simeon and Anna spent their whole lives believing in God and waiting for Him to keep His promise to send His Son. God has promised to send Jesus on Judgment Day to repair His broken creation, to raise the dead, and to give eternal life with Him to you and all believers. Just like Simeon and Anna, you can watch for Jesus' return when you worship God in church, when you read and study your Bible at home and in Sunday School and Bible class, and when you get older, each time you receive Jesus' body and blood in Holy Communion. The Holy Spirit will keep you ready until the day when you can see Jesus' face, just like Simeon and Anna did.

LET'S PRAY: Lord God, thank You for these two older believers who got to see and hold Jesus. Give me such faith and joy all through my life that I may always praise Jesus and tell others what He has done to save us, then be ready to see Him with my own eyes in heaven. In Jesus' name. Amen.

The Visit of the Wise Men

Have you ever been afraid a new boy or girl would come and take your friends away?

When Jesus was born, God His Father put a special star up in the sky. Far away in the East, a group of Wise Men saw it. They gathered gifts together and started following its light. The star led them to the land of Israel. When they reached the big city of Jerusalem, they visited King Herod (HAIR-uhd) and asked where they could find the baby who was born the King of the Jews.

Some people called him Herod the Great because he spent many years improving the temple that the exiles rebuilt when they returned from Babylon. It was beautiful and magnificent. But Herod was a very nervous king. He didn't want anyone to take his kingdom away from him. When the Wise Men said the King of the Jews had been born, he got really scared.

King Herod knew the Jewish people were expecting a Savior. So he asked the priests where the Christ Child was to be born. They read to him the words of the prophet Micah, "And you, O Bethlehem, in the land of Judah, are by no means least among the rulers of Judah; for from you shall come a ruler who will shepherd My people Israel" (see Micah 5:2; Matthew 2:6).

Herod told the Wise Men to go to Bethlehem and search carefully for the child. When they found Him, he wanted them to come back and tell him so he could go and worship Him too. But Herod did not want to worship the baby like they did—he wanted to kill Him!

The Wise Men left Herod and started on their way to Bethlehem. And then they saw the star again. They were extremely happy because they knew they would see this baby king very soon.

You might think Jesus was still lying in the manger, but that was just when He was born. By the time the Wise Men came to Jesus, Matthew tells us Joseph and Mary were living in a house with Jesus. The Wise Men came in and saw Joseph and Mary and the child Jesus. They opened their treasures and gave Jesus gold, frankincense, and myrrh. When God warned them not to go back to Herod, they went back to their country by a different route. Herod was angry when the Wise Men didn't come back. He decided to kill every baby boy in Bethlehem so he wouldn't lose his kingdom. But Herod was not smarter than God. In a dream, an angel told Joseph to take Jesus and Mary to Egypt because Herod would soon try to kill Him.

They stayed there until an angel told them King Herod the Great was dead and it was safe to take Jesus back to Israel. On the way, Joseph learned Herod's son Archelaus (ark-eh-LAY-us) was ruling over Judea. That made him afraid to take Jesus back to Bethlehem. When God warned him in a dream not to go there, Joseph took Mary and Jesus back to Nazareth. Since Jesus grew up there, most people knew Him as Jesus of Nazareth.

Wouldn't you think everyone would be happy to hear that God's Son was born to be our King? But many people are just like Herod—they want to be their own king or queen. That is really sad because Jesus loves them very much, and He is the only one who can save all of us from our sins and bring us safely to heaven.

LET'S PRAY: Lord God, our heavenly Father, thank You for guiding the Wise Men to Jesus by the Christmas star. Guide me through Your Bible, so I can always be close to Jesus and know that He will always be with me. Amen.

The Boy Jesus in the Temple

If you could go anywhere in the world, where would you go? Why do you want to go there?

Joseph and Mary took little Jesus from Bethlehem and went away to live in Egypt (EE-jipt) because King Herod the Great wanted to kill Jesus (Matthew 2). After Herod died, they returned to Nazareth. Since Jesus grew up there, most people knew Him as Jesus of Nazareth.

It would be fun to read about what kind of a boy Jesus was. What toys did He have? What games did He like to play? What were His friends like? But the Bible tells us only one story from Jesus' childhood, when He was twelve years old.

Like every other year, Joseph took his whole family to Jerusalem for the Feast of the Passover. When Passover had ended, Joseph and Mary started back toward Nazareth, traveling with many families from their town. Jesus wasn't with Joseph and Mary, but they weren't concerned because they thought He was traveling with another family. But at the end of the day, when each family came back together, Jesus was missing. Mary and Joseph searched among their relatives and their friends, but they did not find Him. So with great fear, they rushed back to Jerusalem.

Mary and Joseph searched high and low through the city. They didn't find Him until the third day, when they went back to look in the temple courts. And there He was, sitting with a group of teachers. He was listening to them and asking them questions. They were amazed that a twelve-year-old knew the Scriptures so well.

Mary was upset and asked Jesus, "Son, why have You treated us this way? Behold, Your father and I have been searching for You in great distress." But Jesus asked them, "Why were you looking for Me? Did you not know that I must be in My Father's house?" He was surprised that they didn't think to look for Him at the temple right away. Why didn't they realize that the most important thing in the whole world to Him was talking and learning about God His Father?

If your family was on vacation in a strange city and you wandered off, where would you go? To a shopping mall? a museum? a baseball or football stadium? a park? Or would you go to a church? Jesus knew there is no other place in the whole world as important as the place where we can learn about God and His promises to us. That is why church is so important. That is where we learn about all Jesus did to keep God's promises and save us from our sins. And Sunday School and Bible class are special because there we study the Bible and can ask questions we have about God.

LET'S PRAY: Lord Jesus, thank You for learning God's Word so well and for teaching me how important it is for my faith and my life too. Help me to love reading the Bible all through my life. In Your name. Amen.

John Prepares the Way

What kind of job do you want to have when you grow up?

John the Baptist was living in the wilderness when the word of God came to him. He went into the land around the Jordan River and taught people that they had broken God's Commandments and needed to be baptized to wash their sins away. John wore camel's hair and a leather belt around his waist. Those were the same types of clothes the prophet Elijah had worn.

Large crowds came to John from Jerusalem (jeh-ROO-suh-lem) and Judea to be baptized. But some Pharisees (FAIR-uh-seez) and Sadducees (SAD-joo-seez) came too. These people thought they were so good they didn't need to be baptized. John called them snakes: "You brood of vipers! Who warned you to flee from the wrath to come?" (Matthew 3:7).

He was talking about Judgment Day, when everyone who doesn't believe Jesus is their Savior will be punished in hell. John described them as fruit trees that never bear good fruit. Good fruits are the good things we say and do for our neighbors because we love God and Jesus has saved us. But without God's forgiveness and faith, the things we do and say can never be good. John warned the Pharisees and Sadducees, "Even now the axe is laid to the root of the trees. Every tree therefore that does not bear good fruit is cut down and thrown into the fire" (Matthew 3:10).

The Jewish leaders in Jerusalem sent some people to ask John why he was preaching and baptizing people. They asked if he was the promised Messiah or Elijah the prophet. John said no. Then he used the words of Isaiah and answered, "I am the voice of one crying out in the wilderness, 'Make straight the way of the Lord'" (John 1:23). John was only the messenger for the promised Savior.

That was the most exciting news John had to tell the people. God's promised Savior was here, and soon He would start teaching His people. John said, "I baptize with water, but among you stands one you do not know, even He who comes after me, the strap of whose sandal I am not worthy to untie" (John 1:26–27).

When you grow up, God might lead you to be a pastor or a teacher—or maybe a doctor or a nurse, a police officer or firefighter. Whatever job God leads you to, the most important thing you will ever do is help people see their sin and know that Jesus is their Savior from that sin. When you read your Bible and devotions at home and go to church and Sunday School or Bible class, God is preparing you for that work.

LET'S PRAY: Lord God, thank You for sending John to prepare the way for Jesus. Open my ears to listen to his message and prepare me for Jesus' coming, that I may talk to others about their Savior so they will be ready for His coming too. In Jesus' name. Amen.

The Baptism of Jesus

What do you think is so special about being baptized?

When Jesus was all grown up, John the Baptist came and baptized many people along the Jordan River. Then one day, he saw Jesus coming to be baptized too. John was surprised that Jesus came. John's Baptism washed away people's sin—the sin deep inside us that makes us say and do bad things. Deep down inside, John knew he was a sinner too. He needed Jesus to save him like all of us do. But John knew Jesus was God's perfect Son who had no sin to wash away. So John told Jesus, "I need to be baptized by You, and do You come to me?"

Look closely in your Bible at Matthew 3:15 and you will notice Jesus' answer is printed in red. All of His words will be. Jesus told John this was part of God's plan. God the Father sent Jesus into the world to save us from our sin. God sent Him to the Jordan River that day to join His Baptism with ours. In the water of the Jordan, He would take all our sin away from us, put it on His own shoulders, and carry it to the cross, where He would be punished instead of us. After Jesus told John this Baptism was part of God's plan, John agreed and baptized Jesus.

Right away after Jesus was baptized, John watched Him come up out of the water. John saw the heavens torn open like a curtain, and he watched the Holy Spirit come down like a dove and come to rest upon Jesus. That is why Jesus is called *Christ*. The word means "to be anointed," that is, to be set apart by God for an important job. The Holy Spirit would guide Jesus to do everything God His Father wanted Him to do.

Then John heard a loud voice from heaven say, "This is My beloved Son, with whom I am well pleased." That was the voice of God the Father—Jesus' Father—telling John He was very happy with the way Jesus lived His life as a child and a young man. Jesus did it for all of us—so when He took our sin upon Himself in Baptism, He put His holy life on all of us.

Jesus' Baptism makes your Baptism special. When you were baptized, you were joined to Jesus, and Jesus was joined to you. He took away your sin and gave you His perfect life. He made you His own brother or sister, God's own son or daughter. He gave you His Holy Spirit. He made you part of His Church to teach the world about how Jesus saved us by living, dying, and rising to life again.

Because of our Baptism, we are called *Christians*, a word that means "little Christs." God gave us His Holy Spirit to guide us through our lives too. And when you stand before God on Judgment Day, He will see no sin, only Jesus' perfect life. He will be happy to bring you into heaven forever. That is what your Baptism does for you.

LET'S PRAY: Lord God, heavenly Father, thank You for sending Jesus to be baptized and making me Your own child when You baptized me. Give me Your Holy Spirit that I may be ready to tell other people about Your great love. In Jesus' name. Amen.

The Temptation of Jesus

When you are tempted, part of you wants to do something you know is wrong. What temptations are hard for you to say no to?

Right after Jesus was baptized, the Holy Spirit led Him into the wilderness. God the Father wanted to give us a "do-over."

Back in the Garden of Eden, the devil tempted Eve, and both Adam and Eve ate the fruit God commanded them not to eat. Their sin passed on to you and me, making us sinners who should die and receive God's punishment. In this story, Jesus took Adam and Eve's place. If He passed the test without sinning, His obedience would pass on to you and me by faith.

Jesus spent forty days and nights in the wilderness not eating a single thing. At the end, He was really, really hungry. The devil told Him, "If You are the Son of God, command these stones to become loaves of bread."

Do you think part of Jesus was hungry enough to want bread right away? Yes, but using words from the Bible, Jesus answered, "Man shall not live by bread alone, but by every word that comes from the mouth of God." Yes, Jesus was very hungry, but He trusted His heavenly Father to feed Him when the time was right.

Then Satan took Jesus to the top of the temple. He said, "If You are the Son of God, throw Yourself down, for it is written, 'He will command His angels concerning you,' and 'On their hands they will bear you up, lest you strike your foot against a stone.'"

Satan was tricky. If Jesus didn't jump, it would look like He didn't trust His Father's Bible promises!

But Jesus knew that if you really trust God, you never make Him prove He keeps His promises. Using the Bible again, Jesus answered, "Again it is written, 'You shall not put the Lord your God to the test.'"

Finally, Satan took Jesus to a high mountain and showed Him all the kingdoms of the world. Jesus could be king of the whole world if He just bowed down and worshiped Satan.

Do you think part of Jesus might have wanted to do that instead of going to the cross to suffer and die? But Jesus didn't choose the easy way. He answered, "Be gone, Satan! For it is written, 'You shall worship the Lord your God and Him only shall you serve.'"

Since the Son of God commanded him to leave, Satan went away and waited for another time to tempt Him. God the Father sent angels to feed Jesus and take care of Him.

Sometimes, part of you really wants something God doesn't want you to have right now—or maybe ever. Learn the Bible like Jesus did, and the Holy Spirit will give you the strength to say no or wait until God's time is right. But if you fail and sin, like all of us do, remember that Jesus took your sins when He baptized you and paid their price on the cross. Pray to Him, and you will be forgiven.

LET'S PRAY: Lord Jesus, thank You for not giving in to the devil's temptations. Forgive me when I do. Amen.

Jesus Calls Four Disciples

Mark 1:16–20

If you could go on an adventure, where would you want to go?

After Jesus was baptized, He went up to Galilee (GAL-ih-lee). (Galilee is a region in the northern part of Israel.) It was time to start teaching the people of Israel about God's love and how He had come to save them from their sins.

But Jesus knew His time to preach would be really, really short, only a few years. After He died, rose again, and went back to heaven, how would people like you and me learn about Him? So Jesus chose people to follow Him and learn from Him. We call them disciples. Jesus taught these men so they could lead the Church, write the books of the New Testament, and train people to be pastors and teachers after He returned to heaven.

One day, Jesus was walking along the Sea of Galilee. He met two brothers, Simon Peter and Andrew, who were throwing a net into the sea to go fishing. Jesus told them, "Follow Me, and I will make you fishers of men." Right away, they left their nets and started following Him.

A little farther down the beach, He met two other brothers, James and John. They were sitting in their boat, repairing the nets. Every morning when thc fishing was done for the day, fishermen took time to fix their nets so they would be ready for the next catch. Jesus called James and John to follow Him, and they left their father, Zebedee, and his servants in the boat, and they followed Jesus with Peter and Andrew.

This was the start of a tremendous adventure for Peter, Andrew, James, and John. These men would hear Jesus' wonderful words and see His amazing miracles. They would travel with Him all through the land of Israel. They would ride in boats with Him. They would eat and sleep beside Him. They would watch Him die on the cross and rise again. And with the Holy Spirit guiding them, they would write about the things they saw and heard. Those writings are in the New Testament.

When you were baptized, God started you on a wonderful adventure. You may not be able to follow Jesus around like Peter, Andrew, James, and John could. But whenever you read your Bible, you are right there with Jesus and them, listening to His words and seeing the amazing things He did—especially dying on the cross to save you from your sin.

Jesus promised to be right there beside you every day, protecting you from harm and giving you everything you need. He has promised to control everything that happens to you and make it work to bring you closer to Him. And at the end of the adventure, you will be with God your Father and Jesus your Savior forever and ever. What better adventure could you ever hope for?

LET'S PRAY: Lord Jesus, thank You for calling Your first four disciples to leave their lives of fishing and follow You on a great adventure. Thank You for calling me in my Baptism. Forgive my sins, and give me great joy and confidence each day of my adventure through this life toward heaven. In Your name. Amen.

Jesus Changes Water into Wine

When you have a big problem, how do you try to solve it?

Early in Jesus' ministry, He was invited to a wedding in a town called Cana. His mother, Mary, had been invited too. Jesus brought along the disciples He had gathered.

Back in those days, wedding celebrations lasted many days. But very early in this party, Mary learned there was a big problem. They had run out of wine. She knew how embarrassed the bride and groom and their families would be if the guests found out. Mary took that problem to Jesus and taught us something very important. She told Jesus, "They have no wine." She didn't tell Jesus how she thought He should solve the problem—she just told Him what the problem was, and then she left it up to Him to decide the best way to take care of it.

Jesus answered, "Woman, what does this have to do with Me? My hour has not yet come." Jesus was looking toward to Good Friday, when He would die on the cross, when He would show the world just how much He loves all people.

Mary trusted Jesus. She told the servants, "Do whatever He tells you."

Jesus told the servants to go fill six large jars clear to the top with water. When the jars were full, Jesus told the servants to draw some out and take it to the master of the feast. The master of the feast was the guy who made sure all the wedding guests had all the food and drink they needed.

The servants did exactly what Jesus said. As they were carrying the water to the master, Jesus used His mighty power to work His first miracle. He turned that water into wine.

When the master of the feast tasted the new wine, he was impressed at how delicious it was. He told the new husband that at most wedding feasts they serve the good wine first. Then, when the guests have been drinking, they bring out wine that is not so good. But he was impressed because this husband saved the best wine for last.

The most amazing thing about this sign, which very few knew about, is that when Jesus had shown His glory, His disciples believed in Him.

With this sign, Jesus directs us (those who hear and read John's account) to His final sign of the cross. So when we call on the Father to help us, the sign of Jesus' death is the proof that He will care for us in every other way. In this way, our Father invites us to pray boldly to Him as dear children ask their fathers. He loves us as a husband dearly loves his bride.

LET'S PRAY: Lord Jesus, thank You for making delicious new wine for the new husband and wife. Remind us that You care about everything in our lives—no matter how big or how small. Help me to teach others about Your great love and kindness. Amen.

The Sermon on the Mount

How do you think Jesus wants you to treat other children? Why is it hard to do that sometimes?

Jesus went from village to village, telling people about God's love. Large groups of people from all over came to follow Him. One day, they followed Him up onto a mountain, where they all sat down and He began to teach them.

First, He promised forgiveness for those who were sorry for their sins. Jesus said they would live in the new heavens and earth when He came back on Judgment Day. He promised a special blessing to His believers who are treated badly because they love Jesus.

Then Jesus said, "You are the light of the world." That's how we are when we are kind, gentle, and patient with other people. Like a bright light on a dark night, we show that God's love is inside us, and when other people feel that love, some of them will want to know more about Jesus' love.

Next, Jesus talked about the Ten Commandments. Many people think they will go to heaven because they are pretty good and do many good things. But Jesus said being good part of the time isn't good enough for God. We have to be perfect all the time. To show us what He meant, He talked about the commandment "you shall not kill."

Many people think they keep this commandment because they haven't killed anyone. But God looks deep in our hearts and minds. Whenever we hate others and wish they were dead, we break this commandment—even when we hold on to our anger and refuse to forgive them for something bad they did to us. Jesus was teaching us that no matter how hard we try, we are sinners and we will always need His forgiveness, power, and help. So next He taught us how to pray.

Jesus taught us a special prayer we call the Lord's Prayer. It reminds us that God is our Father, who loves us very much. When we pray to Him, we can be sure He will forgive our sins and give us every good thing we really need.

Many people worry they will not have enough food, clothes, or other things to be able to live. Jesus reminds us that God feeds His birds and dresses His flowers to look beautiful—even weeds. He loves us more than birds and plants, so we can be sure He will take care of everything we need.

Jesus ended His sermon with a neat picture. He said if we listen closely and do the things He taught, we will be like a wise person who built his house on a rock. When the rain falls and the wind blows and the water rises, the house will stand strong and secure. But if we don't do what He said, we will be like a foolish person who built his house on sand. When the rain falls, the wind blows, and the water rises, the house will fall with a mighty crash.

LET'S PRAY: Loving Father, thank You for Jesus' wonderful words that teach us how to live. Forgive me when I do wrong, and help me trust You, pray to You, and serve You every way I can. In Jesus' name. Amen.

Jesus Calms a Storm

Mark 4:35–41

What kind of weather scares you most?

Jesus went all through Galilee teaching people and healing those who couldn't see, hear, walk, or use their arms. He also healed people who were sick. So many people came to Him that He got really tired, and so did His disciples.

One day, He decided they needed to get away and be by themselves for a little while so they could rest. He got into a boat with all His disciples to go across the Sea of Galilee. Other boats went along with them. Jesus was so tired that He lay down on a cushion in the back of the boat and fell fast asleep.

While He was sleeping, a strong windstorm rose up over the sea. The wind was blowing really hard, and it made the waves grow taller and taller. The waves became so high that they crashed over the side of the boat and started filling it up with water. The disciples watched as the boat sank lower and lower. But when they looked at Jesus, He was sleeping like a baby.

Many of Jesus' disciples were fishermen. They had grown up on this water and had gone through storms before. But this one was really bad. Their boat was filling with water, and they knew it wouldn't be long before it sank. With the huge waves, they didn't think they would be able to swim to the shore when the boat went down. They grew very scared and they woke Jesus, saying, "Teacher, do You not care that we are perishing?"

Jesus woke up and spoke to the wind and sea as if they were children. He commanded them, "Peace! Be still!" Right away, the wind stopped and the sea was completely calm; the waves were gone. Jesus turned to His disciples and asked, "Why are you so afraid? Have you still no faith?"

Everyone on the boat was shocked. Storms just don't stop because a person stands and shouts for them to stop. They said to one another, "Who then is this, that even the wind and the sea obey Him?" More and more, Jesus was showing His disciples He wasn't just a normal man like they were. He was God's Son.

Sometimes, the weather gets bad and we get scared. Lightning, thunder, strong winds, and loud hail are very frightening. Other times, we might get sick, or someone may want to hurt us. But Jesus is the mighty Son of God who created the heavens and the earth. He is in control of the weather and everything that happens on earth. He has promised to take care of us always. And we can trust His promise because He went to the cross to suffer and die for our sins, and He rose to life again on the third day.

LET'S PRAY: Lord Jesus, thank You for showing Your power over the winds and the waves that You created. Whenever I'm scared of storms or other things in my life, remind me that You are in complete control, and I am safe in Your hands. Amen.

Jesus Calls Matthew

Is there a bully at your school? Describe what that person is like.

Jesus went through the land of Israel teaching people. One day, He stopped at a tax booth in the road. People had to stop at the booth to pay money to the government when they wanted to sell fish, clothes, or other things to people. It's like the taxes your parents pay when they buy things at the store.

In Jesus' time, people didn't like tax collectors at all. The collectors often took more money than they were supposed to. They were like bullies on a playground—no one could tell them to stop because Roman soldiers stood by them and threatened to beat up anyone who wouldn't pay the taxes.

Matthew was the tax collector sitting at the booth that day. Jesus told him, "Follow Me." Right away, Matthew got up, left the taxes behind, and started following Jesus.

That confused the crowds. They liked Jesus before, but now He was choosing people they hated and inviting them to be His disciples too. They weren't sure how to think about Jesus anymore—should they keep following Him?

Jesus loved them, but He loved the tax collectors too. He wanted to wash away all their sins and give them heaven. He also wanted to change them so they would stop being greedy and selfish and start treating people fairly.

Matthew was so happy, he held a big party for Jesus and the other apostles at his house. His house was filled with tax collectors and other sinners that most people did not like. Together, they had a wonderful time talking to Jesus and learning how much God loved them.

The next day, Matthew left his tax booth behind and followed Jesus as one of the twelve disciples. After Jesus died and rose again, Matthew wrote the very first of the four Gospels, this book that teaches us so much about Jesus. He wrote it especially for the Jews, the people who once hated him for being a tax collector. What kinder thing could he have ever done for them?

Can you imagine Jesus going up to a bully on your playground and telling him He loves him, wants to forgive him, and wants to lead him to heaven? What would you think? What would the other children think who have been beaten up by him? Jesus changes people—even bullies. When they follow Him, He forgives all their sin—even the times they bullied others. He helps them be kind, caring, and helpful.

Do you know how Jesus goes up to bullies and talks to them today? He does it through you and me, when we go up to them and show them God's love and kindness. He does it when we forgive them and treat them nicely. That is very hard to do. It takes God's love and a lot of prayers. But think how wonderful that would be for everyone at your school if the bullies stopped bullying and played nice!

LET'S PRAY: Lord Jesus, thank You for caring about people who get picked on by bullies—and also for caring about the bullies too. Teach me to be kind and loving to everyone—even my bullies—so everyone can see Your love shining like a bright light inside me. Amen.

Jesus Raises Jairus's Daughter

Mark 5:21–24, 35–43

Have you ever been really, really sick?

One day while Jesus was teaching a large crowd, a man named Jairus (JIGH-ruhs) came up to Him. He was very scared and needed Jesus' help very, very badly. He fell on his knees before Jesus and begged Him, "My little daughter is at the point of death. Come and lay Your hands on her, so that she may be made well and live." Jesus and His disciples went with Jairus.

But while they were on their way, some people came from Jairus's house. They told him, "Your daughter is dead. Why trouble the Teacher any further?" When Jesus overheard what they said, He told Jairus, "Do not fear; only believe."

When they got to the house, it was full of people weeping and crying. Jesus asked them why they were carrying on that way. He told them, "The child is not dead but sleeping." But they knew she was dead. They knew that no matter how loudly someone yelled at her or how hard they shook her, she would never wake up. They started laughing at Jesus like He was crazy.

Jesus made them all go outside. Taking along only three of His disciples—Peter, James, and John—Jesus went into the girl's bedroom with Jairus and the girl's mother. Jesus reached out and took hold of the child's hand. He said to her, "Little girl, I say to you, arise."

If Jairus or his wife had tried to do that, she would have stayed dead. But Jesus is the Son of God. When He spoke to her, she immediately sat up, got up out of bed, and started walking around. Jesus told her parents and His three disciples not to tell anyone what had happened. Then He told Jairus and his wife to give her something to eat. Peter, James, and John were amazed and remembered this for a long, long time. In fact, years later when Mark wrote about this miracle, he wrote down the very words Jesus had said to the girl: "Talitha cumi."

Sometimes, girls and boys get really sick. And sometimes, like Jairus's daughter, they even die. But we never have to be afraid of dying, because Jesus died on the cross to take away our sin. He was laid in a tomb, but death was not strong enough to hold the Son of God and keep Him in that tomb. On the third day, Jesus rose from the dead and left the tomb empty.

Death can't hold us, either, because when Jesus comes back on Judgment Day, He will raise up all the dead just as easily as He raised Jairus's daughter. That is why Jesus said the child was not dead but sleeping. That is why the Bible often describes death as sleep—because Jesus will wake us to eternal life when He comes again. Then all of us who trust in Him as our Savior will live with Him forever.

LET'S PRAY: Lord Jesus, thank You for showing us Your power over death. Whenever we are afraid, remind us that You are bigger than any problem we could ever have. Make us ready for the day You return to take us to live with You forever. Amen.

Jesus Heals Two Blind Men

Matthew 9:27–31

Have you ever prayed for something but God didn't do what you asked?

One day, two blind men followed Jesus around, calling out, "Have mercy on us, Son of David." They believed Jesus was the Messiah, the Savior God had promised to raise up from one of King David's sons.

Today is very different from that time. There are many different kinds of jobs people can do today, even if they can't see. But at the time Jesus lived on earth, there weren't jobs for people who couldn't see, so these men couldn't work to take care of their families and community. There was nothing they could do to make their eyes work. But they believed Jesus could heal them.

Jesus waited to talk to them until they followed Him into the house. He didn't want everyone in the crowd to see this miracle. He turned to them and asked, "Do you believe I am able to do this?" They answered, "Yes, Lord."

Since Jesus is God, He didn't have to wait until they believed in Him before He could heal them. But He wanted them to understand how important their faith was. When Jesus died on the cross, He paid for everyone's sins. But only those who believe in Him will go to heaven. That's how important faith is. So after the blind men told Him they had faith and believed, Jesus touched them and said, "According to your faith be it done to you." Right away, they were able to see.

Of course, they were really, really excited. But Jesus commanded them, "See that no one knows about this." Jesus did not want them to go out and tell everyone that He had healed them. The Jewish people were expecting the Messiah to come and throw out the Roman armies, make Israel free, and make their lives perfect. They did not understand the Old Testament prophets who said the Messiah must suffer and die to take away their sins and make them right with God. Only after He died and rose again would His followers finally understand why He came. Then they would be free to talk about all the miracles they saw.

Jesus taught us two things by healing the blind men. First, He cares very much about things that hurt us and make our lives hard. He won't always solve our problems right away, but He hears our prayers and works for us.

The second thing is how important our faith is. God has the power to do anything we could ever ask—and He cares about us and promises to answer every prayer. The Holy Spirit gives us faith to believe these things about God. But remember one more thing—God is smarter than we are. Sometimes He chooses a better way to answer our prayers than we can think of. When God doesn't do it the way we want, we may feel like He doesn't hear or care. But Jesus' cross proves that is not true. Our God is good, powerful, and loving. He will take care of every problem we will ever have and make everything work for the best.

LET'S PRAY: Lord Jesus, when You healed the two blind men, You showed Your care and kindness for each of us. Give me faith that whenever I have problems and pray to You, You will hear my prayer and do what is best for me. Amen.

Jesus Feeds Five Thousand Mark 6:30–44

Describe a time you couldn't do something because you were too young or too little.

Jesus and His disciples were very busy. Huge crowds of people kept gathering to hear Him preach and to be healed of their sicknesses. Finally, Jesus told His disciples, "Come away by yourselves to a desolate place and rest awhile." They got on a boat and sailed to the other side of the Sea of Galilee to a place where nobody lived.

But the Sea of Galilee isn't a very big lake. The crowds saw Jesus sail off, so they just walked around the lake to meet Him on the other side. When Jesus and His disciples reached the shore, a huge crowd was waiting for Him!

Jesus looked at their faces, and He knew why they had come. He knew they were hurting and scared. They didn't know if God loved them or if He was going to punish them. So instead of turning around in the boat or ordering the crowds to leave, Jesus welcomed them and began teaching them.

He healed the sick, and He taught and preached all day long. Before the disciples knew it, the sun was getting low in the sky and it was nearly suppertime. They looked around and realized there were no cities on that side of the lake, no places for the people to go and buy food. They urged Jesus to send the crowds away so they could go and find food. But Jesus told them the people didn't need to go away. He said, "You give them something to eat."

The disciples looked at the huge crowd and said, "We only have five loaves here and two fish." That was probably not even enough food for Jesus and the Twelve—it never would have been enough for all those people.

Jesus told them, "Bring the food here to Me." He told the people to sit down in groups on the grass. He took the food, looked up to heaven, and prayed for God His Father to bless it. Then He began handing it to His disciples. They took it from Jesus' hands and started passing it out to the crowds. Jesus kept handing bread and fish to the disciples, and they kept passing it out to the people until everyone was full. Then Jesus told His disciples to gather up all the leftover food so none of it would be wasted. They ended up gathering more leftover food than the five loaves and two fish Jesus started with.

Sometimes, we have to do things that seem too hard. We aren't tall enough, fast enough, smart enough, or strong enough. We don't have enough time or money. But Jesus is able to take what we have and make it more. So whenever you don't know what to do, just look to Jesus and ask Him to help. He'll always be there for you.

LET'S PRAY: Lord Jesus, thank You for reminding us that You will always give us everything we need. Help us to trust You so we can spend our time helping other people instead of worrying about ourselves. Amen.

Jesus Walks on Water

Have you ever had to do something you thought you could never do?

It had been a long, long day for the twelve disciples. After Jesus spent all day teaching, He fed a huge crowd with a little bread and a few fish. Then while He stayed back to send the crowds home and pray, He made the disciples get in a boat and row to the other side of the sea. But they were having a tough time because the wind was blowing hard against them. They had been rowing most of the night, but they still hadn't reached the other shore.

Suddenly, they saw something that scared them to death. Someone or something was walking across the water right at them! They cried out in fear, "It is a ghost!"

But it wasn't a ghost—it was Jesus! He told them, "Take heart; it is I. Do not be afraid." He was right there— the Son of God was walking across the top of the water toward them! Their fear turned to happiness. Peter said, "Lord, if it is You, command me to come to You on the water." Peter knew he couldn't walk on water by himself— but Jesus could give him the power to do it. Jesus told him, "Come."

Peter stood up, stepped over the side of the boat and down onto the water, and it worked— the water held him up! He took a few steps and sure enough, the water held firm under him just like he was walking across the ground. He started walking to Jesus.

But then Peter looked around. He felt the wind blowing, saw the waves, and got scared. He remembered that people can't walk on water, and as his faith got replaced by doubt and fear, he quickly sank into the waves. Looking to Jesus, he cried out, "Lord, save me." Right away, Jesus reached out and took him by the hand. He pulled Peter back on top of the water and said, "O you of little faith, why did you doubt?"

Peter held tight to Jesus' hand, and they walked together to the boat.

When they got into the boat, the winds stopped blowing. The twelve disciples in the boat were shocked and amazed. They bowed and fell down at Jesus' feet and said, "Truly You are the Son of God."

Sometimes we have to do really hard things, things that seem impossible, like maybe trying to figure out something new in math, going to the hospital for a scary surgery, or going out to the playground where someone is being really mean. But Jesus is always right here with us, and nothing is too hard for Him. He has the power to help us do anything we need to do. And the good news is that even when we have doubts and get really scared, Jesus is right there, reaching out to hold us safely in His strong hand. He can pick us back up and keep us safe while He walks with us through our problems and worries.

LET'S PRAY: Lord Jesus, thank You for being there for Peter when he started doubting. Thank You for being there for me when I get scared. Make my faith strong to know You will always be here for me. Amen.

Jesus Heals Many

Have you ever gone to the doctor's office and looked around at the people sitting in the waiting room? What clues could help you guess what is hurting them?

In the Gospels, the books about Jesus' life on earth, we read many times where Jesus healed a blind man or a deaf person, raised a dead girl to life again, or drove a demon out of a boy. It is easy to think that Jesus healed only a few people at a time, here or there. But the Gospels tell us about times when huge crowds came to Jesus bringing many, many people who were sick and hurting—and Jesus healed them all.

One of those times happened when Jesus was walking along the Sea of Galilee. Matthew tells us what he saw: "Great crowds came to Him, bringing with them the lame, the blind, the crippled, the mute, and many others, and they put them at His feet, and He healed them."

Lame people are people who are too weak to walk. Blind people cannot see. Crippled people have weak or bent arms or legs and can't walk or do things with their hands. Mute people are unable to talk.

The crowds brought these sick people to Jesus because they had heard how He had healed sick people in other towns. And Jesus healed every single person who was brought to Him. And this didn't happen just once—it happened many, many times during His ministry, when He went around teaching about God's kingdom before He died on the cross.

We read in the Old Testament about how God worked through prophets to heal a few people—especially through the prophets Elijah and Elisha. But Jesus was healing great crowds of people in many different places! This is exactly what God's Old Testament prophets said the Messiah would do when He came. All these healing miracles made it clear that Jesus was that Messiah, whom God had promised to Adam and Eve. When the crowds saw Jesus healing everyone who came to Him, they were amazed and said great things about God.

When you get sick and see the doctor, most times you don't feel good right away. The doctor may give you some pills, but sometimes it takes a few days before you start feeling better. Some children have to have surgery where the doctor goes in and fixes something in their bodies that isn't working right. That takes even longer to feel better.

But when people came to Jesus, He made them feel good right away— no medicine, no surgery. Remember, Jesus didn't come just to heal sick bodies, though. He came to take away our sins on the cross and to save us from hell. When you were baptized, He took your sins away and promised you eternal life with Him in heaven. When He comes again, He will heal our bodies perfectly, all at once. Then we will live with Jesus forever, never ever to get sick again.

LET'S PRAY: Lord Jesus, thank You for caring about all the people who came to You and healing so many who were sick. When my body isn't working right and I don't feel well, remind me that You are here. And when You return, You will make my body perfect forever. Amen.

Jesus Is Rejected at Nazareth Luke 4:16–30

What are some Bible stories you've heard over and over again?

After Jesus was baptized, He went through the towns in Galilee doing many mighty miracles—healing people who were hurting, raising the dead, even driving out demons. The news spread, and people came from all the nearby towns to hear Him and see Him. Now, it was time for Jesus to go back home to Nazareth, the town where He grew up and worked in Joseph's carpenter shop.

The people of Nazareth had heard about all the wonderful things Jesus was doing. They invited Him to come and speak in their synagogue (SINN-uh-gog), their church. So Jesus stood up to read from Isaiah. He read, "The Spirit of the Lord is upon Me, because He has anointed Me to proclaim good news to the poor. He has sent Me to proclaim liberty to the captives and recovering of sight to the blind, to set free those who are oppressed, to proclaim the year of the Lord's favor."

Jesus started to preach and said, "Today this Scripture has been fulfilled in your hearing." He told His friends and neighbors that He was the Savior God had promised to send them.

At first, the people of Nazareth were excited to listen to the wonderful things Jesus was saying, and they really respected Him. But then they started thinking about all those years Jesus had lived there as a boy and a young man. They had never seen Him heal someone who was sick or drive out a demon or raise someone who was dead. They only saw Him working in Joseph's carpenter shop or sweeping the floor at the end of the day. They got mad and refused to believe He could be the promised Savior.

Jesus heard them grumbling against Him, and He told them they were as stubborn as the people in Elijah and Elisha's time. Since so many Israelites had refused to believe Elijah and Elisha, God did not let the prophets do miracles for many Israelites, but mostly for some Gentile neighbors.

When Jesus told the people of Nazareth He was not going to heal their sick, that really made them mad. They grabbed Him and carried Him to a very high cliff on the edge of their town. They were going to throw Him off the cliff to kill Him. But Jesus used His mighty power to pass right through them, and He went away.

When you grow up going to church, you hear the same stories of things Jesus said and did many, many times, over and over again. When you get older, it can be easy to think, "Oh, I've heard that before," and then stop listening and paying attention—and in time, stop believing in Jesus. That is why we need to listen very closely whenever we hear or read the stories about Jesus' life, His death, and His resurrection. That is why we pray to the Holy Spirit to keep us believing and loving Jesus, our Savior.

LET'S PRAY: Jesus, it is sad when people get so used to hearing about You that they stop noticing how great, kind, and wonderful You are. Help me never get tired of hearing about You. Make my faith strong and alive every day of my life. Amen.

Jesus Drives Out Demons

Luke 8:26–39

What do you think a demon is like?

Once, Jesus sailed across the Sea of Galilee in a boat with His disciples. When He got out on the other side, He was met by a man who had a demon.

Demons are bad angels who hate God and hate us. They weren't that way when God first created them. At first, they were all good and holy and kind. So was their leader, the angel we now call the devil. But that powerful angel turned against God and convinced a lot of angels to join him against God. We call these bad, fallen angels demons.

The demon inside this man made him very dangerous, so the rulers put him in chains. But the demon made the man so strong that he broke the chains, and no one could control him. The demon made him live far away from other people—he stayed in the places where dead people were buried. Everyone was so afraid they stayed far away from him.

When Jesus landed, the demon made the man come up to Him and shout as loudly as he could, "What have You to do with me, Jesus, Son of the Most High God? I beg You not to torment me." These really bad angels knew the Son of God, and they were afraid of Him. They knew Jesus had come to earth to destroy their works. They knew that one day God would punish them for all the bad things they had done.

Jesus asked the demon his name, and it said "Legion." This was the name the Roman army gave to a group of four thousand to six thousand soldiers, so there were thousands of demons living together inside this man. Jesus commanded them to leave the man. They begged Him to let them go into a herd of pigs that was feeding nearby. Jesus let them go. The demons entered the pigs and made them all rush off the cliff into the Sea of Galilee, where they all died. This scared the people of that land, and they begged Jesus to leave them. So He got ready to get back in the boat and sail over to the other side.

The man was now free of the demons. He came up to thank Jesus and asked if he could follow Him. Instead, Jesus told him to stay and tell his neighbors everything God had done for him. He obeyed Jesus, and his neighbors were amazed when they heard about Jesus driving out all those demons.

The devil and his bad angels can be very scary—until we realize how much stronger Jesus is. When He died on the cross, He set us free from their tricks and their power. When He returns again, He will send them to hell forever, and they will never escape to tempt us or bother us ever again. Until then, He sends us holy angels to guard and protect us, so we don't ever have to be afraid the devil or his demons will come into us and take control.

LET'S PRAY: Lord Jesus, even the bad angels have to obey You when You give them commands. Take away any fear I have of them, so I can trust You and show Your love to the people around me. Amen.

The Good Samaritan
Luke 10:25–37

Which kids at school are the hardest for you to be nice to? Why?

Many Jewish teachers were telling people the only way they could get to heaven was to carefully follow a list of rules or laws the teachers had made up. That is why they were called "lawyers." One of these lawyers asked Jesus what a person had to do to get into heaven.

Jesus asked him, "What is written in the Law? How do you read it?" Jesus was talking about God's Ten Commandments.

The lawyer answered, "You shall love the Lord your God with all your heart and with all your soul and with all your strength and with all your mind, and your neighbor as yourself." These are God's words that show how to keep His Ten Commandments.

Jesus told him, "You have answered correctly; do this, and you will live."

The teacher was proud. Maybe he didn't love all people as much as he loved himself, but if only certain people counted as his neighbor, he could certainly get into heaven on his own. He asked Jesus, "Who is my neighbor?"

So Jesus told a story about a Jewish man who was walking down the road from Jerusalem to Jericho. Thieves beat him, stole his clothes and possessions, and left him half dead. This poor man was going to die unless someone stopped and helped him.

Two Jewish leaders went by—a priest and a Levite. Both of them saw the beaten man, but they walked to the other side of the road and passed by like they had never seen him. Then a Samaritan came along. The Jews hated the Samaritans and treated them badly. But when this Samaritan looked at the dying Jewish man, he felt sorry for him, and he stopped to take care of him.

Jesus asked the teacher, "Which of these three, do you think, proved to be a neighbor to the man?" The teacher said it was the Samaritan because he stopped to take care of him. Jesus told him to go and do the same: Treat every single person as if he or she were his neighbor—even people he didn't like and people who didn't like him.

Some people hear this parable of the Good Samaritan and think Jesus was teaching that if we just love people and treat everyone like our neighbor, we can get to heaven without faith in Him. But He was showing that none of us keeps God's rules. None of us loves God more than everything else, and none of us loves every other person as much as we love ourselves. Think about the boy or girl at school who picks on you or makes fun of you. Do you love him or her as much as you love yourself? The only way we can be saved is by trusting in Jesus, who loved every one of us enough to take our sins and die on the cross in our place.

LET'S PRAY: Lord Jesus, I can't keep all of God's Commandments perfectly. Thank You for coming to earth to keep those rules for me and for dying on the cross to take away the punishment I deserve for breaking them. Amen.

The Lord's Prayer

Luke 11:1–13

How would you teach a friend to pray?

Jesus prayed a lot. He prayed when He woke up in the morning, before and after He ate, and when He went to bed. Jesus got up early some mornings to pray—and stayed up really late some nights. Sometimes, He never went to bed at all because He was praying.

The disciples asked Jesus, "Lord, teach us to pray." Jesus taught them a special prayer, a prayer we use in church every single week, a prayer you should pray every day. It goes like this:

Our Father who art in heaven. God made you His own son or daughter when He baptized you. Since He is in heaven, He can give you everything you could ask for.

Hallowed be Thy name. Hallowed means "holy," and God's name is His reputation—what people think about Him. We ask God to help us trust that He is good and perfect—and to help us teach that to others.

Thy kingdom come. God is our King. When Jesus comes back, He will send away everyone that refuses to serve Him and believe in Him. We ask Him to make us ready for that day by faith, and to help us warn others so they will believe in Jesus and always be ready.

Thy will be done on earth as it is in heaven. In heaven, the holy angels always do everything God tells them to do. We thank God for saving us through Jesus, and we ask Him to help us love Him and all other people as He wants.

Give us this day our daily bread. Jesus teaches us to ask God for our food, clothes, family, friends, and everything we need to live.

And forgive us our trespasses as we forgive those who trespass against us. We ask God to forgive us for Jesus' sake for the times we break His rules. We ask God to help us forgive people who sin against us.

And lead us not into temptation. The devil, people around us, and our own sinful nature tempt us to do bad things. We ask God to help us say no and do what God wants.

But deliver us from evil. We ask God to protect us from the devil's plans and keep our faith strong so we will always believe in Jesus and be ready for Him to come again.

That was the end of the prayer Jesus taught His disciples. In church, we add a few more words at the end to thank Jesus and to remind us God will always answer our prayers:

For Thine is the kingdom and the power and the glory, forever and ever. Amen. God is our great King who has the power to do everything we need. The word "Amen" says we believe God will answer our prayers for Jesus' sake.

In this great prayer, Jesus gives us just the right words to pray to God our Father so we can be sure He will give us what we need, all for Jesus' sake. Amen.

LET'S PRAY: Lord Jesus, thank You for Your wonderful prayer. Remind me that You always hear me and that Your Father loves me as His own child. Then I can pray and know that You will give me what is best. Amen.

The Prodigal Son Luke 15:11–32

How do you feel about the children at school who break the rules and get into trouble a lot?

Jewish lawyers taught people they had to keep rules to get to heaven. The Pharisees were people who looked up to these lawyers and tried to keep all their rules.

Most Pharisees were proud of themselves and hated people who broke the rules. They thought tax collectors and sinners would never go to heaven. So when they saw Jesus eating and drinking with these rule breakers, they grumbled and complained.

Jesus told them a story about a dad who had two sons. The younger son asked his dad to give him a lot of money. Then he moved far away where he could break his father's rules and do whatever he wanted. He spent all that money doing bad things. But when his money was gone, things turned really bad. He had no job, no food, no home, no friends. The only work he could find was feeding food scraps to pigs. He was so hungry, he would have eaten those nasty, stinky scraps—but no one cared or gave him anything.

Then he started thinking about home. He thought of how hungry he was, and how his father's servants had more than enough to eat. Knowing he didn't deserve to be treated like a son anymore, he decided to go home, tell his dad he was wrong, and ask if he could become one of the servants.

But when his dad saw him walking home, he loved him and ran out to him. He hugged him, put new clothes on him, and had a big feast to welcome him home—not as a servant, but as his son.

The older brother heard about it, and he was upset. Like the Pharisees seeing Jesus eating with the rule breakers who came back to God, he refused to join the celebration. So the father went out and begged him to come in. But the older son complained that he always kept his father's rules and never disobeyed, but he was never given a meal to celebrate with his friends.

The problem was the older son didn't really know his father at all. He thought he was a mean dad who only loved his children if they kept all the rules. But a good father does not love his children like that. He loves them no matter what—even if they break the rules. Since the younger son returned to his father and confessed his sins, it was right to welcome him back as a full son and celebrate.

It is easy for us to be proud and think we are better than boys and girls who break the rules. But we break God's rules when we sin. Still, God our Father loves us—and He loves them too. Jesus came to suffer and die for them just like He came to suffer and die for us. God wants us to go and tell them He loves them and wants to bring them home to heaven too.

LET'S PRAY: Lord Jesus, teach me to love all boys and girls, even the ones who break all the rules and make my life hard. Teach me what to say to show them Your love and goodness. Amen.

Jesus Heals Ten Lepers

Luke 17:11–19

Have you ever wanted something very, very much for your birthday or Christmas?

Jesus was traveling to Jerusalem. He entered a village and was met by ten lepers. Leprosy was a terrible disease that easily passed from one person to the next. To stop it from spreading as quickly, God required lepers to stay far away from other people. People with leprosy had to leave their villages and towns. Since they could no longer be with their families and friends, lepers often lived together, like these ten.

The lepers stood far away from Jesus and in loud voices called out, "Jesus, Master, have mercy on us." To "have mercy" means to care so much about someone who is suffering that you have to do something to help. Sometimes when Jesus met lepers, He showed His mercy by walking up to them, touching them, and healing them. But this time, Jesus stayed where He was and told them, "Go and show yourselves to the priests." They did what Jesus said and went on their way. While they were going, Jesus healed their leprosy, and they were healthy again.

Nine of the ten were so excited they forgot all about Jesus. Maybe they thought about their families and friends and how wonderful it was going to be to run back and touch them again. Maybe they thought about all the things they could do now that they were healthy again. These nine hurried off and forgot all about Jesus, who had given them back their lives.

But one remembered. He came running back, fell on his face at Jesus' feet, and thanked Him over and over and over again. And the strange thing was that this man was not a Jew like the other nine. He was a Samaritan.

Jesus was happy that he had come back, but He asked about the nine Jews. He said, "Were not ten cleansed? Where are the other nine?

Was no one found to return and give praise to God except this foreigner?" Then He turned to the Samaritan and said, "Rise and go your way; your faith has made you well."

Think about that birthday or Christmas present you had been wanting and waiting for so long. What did you do when you got it? Did you open it up and start playing with it? Did you ever think about the person who gave it to you, stop playing, and say thank you? Many times in your life, God will give you great things. Saying thank You in a prayer will help you remember how good God is to give you so many good things every day.

But sometimes bad things happen—like when you get sick, lose friends, have to move, get hurt or scared or worried. That's when it is good to remember to pray to Jesus to help you. But what happens after He helps you and takes that problem away? Then we need to remember to stop and thank Him for helping us.

LET'S PRAY: Heavenly Father, You have been so good and kind to me and to all people. Forgive me for not always remembering to stop and thank You for all Your kindness to me. Now and each time You answer my prayers, remind me to stop and give You thanks. In Jesus' name. Amen.

193

Jesus Teaches Nicodemus

Why is it important to follow rules?

Pharisees were not full-time church workers like the priests and Levites. They were normal Jews who thought they could gain entrance to God's heavenly home if they were careful to follow all the rules their teachers taught them. Jesus came along and taught them that it did not make God happy when they trusted in their rule-keeping rather than in His love for them. Many of the Pharisees were upset at this and refused to listen to Him.

But some Pharisees listened to Jesus. One was Nicodemus (nick-uh-DEE-muhs), an important Jewish leader and a judge on the highest Jewish court. All the miracles made him believe Jesus was from God. He wanted to talk to Jesus but was scared he would get in trouble if the other judges and leaders saw him with Jesus. So he waited until it was dark outside.

One night, Nicodemus came and told Jesus, "We know You are a teacher come from God, for no one can do these signs that You do unless God is with Him." Jesus answered him, "Truly, truly I say to you, unless one is born again he cannot see the kingdom of God."

Nicodemus tried really hard, but he couldn't understand what Jesus meant when He said one must be "born again." He asked, "How can a man be born when he is old?" Did Jesus mean he had to go back in his mom's tummy and be born a second time?

Jesus answered, "Unless one is born of water and the Spirit, he cannot enter the kingdom of God." Now it was clear. Jesus was talking about God making people new again, as He does in Baptism. Most Pharisees had refused to be baptized. They knew Baptism was to wash away sins. But they didn't think they had any sins to wash away; they thought they were good people who did not need God's work on them.

Jesus told Nicodemus, "What is born of the flesh is flesh, and what is born of the Spirit is spirit." He meant that the first time we were born, we had the same sinful nature our mothers and fathers have. No matter how hard we try to keep the rules, we are not good enough. We all need to have our sins washed away.

Jesus told Nicodemus what gives Baptism its power to wash away sins: "For God so loved the world, that He gave His only Son, that whoever believes in Him should not perish but have eternal life."

Nicodemus was used to following rules. Rules are a good thing when they help us get along with other people and treat one another fairly. But rules can't make us right with God. Only Jesus can do that. God loved each of us so much, He sent Jesus, His Son, to keep the Commandments for us. Then, He punished Jesus on the cross for all the times we break His rules. In Baptism, God washed away your sins and made you His own child for Jesus' sake. Because of Jesus' perfect life, His death on the cross, and His resurrection, you have life with our heavenly Father right now; and you will see God in His own house.

LET'S PRAY: Lord Jesus, thank You for my Baptism, when the Holy Spirit gave me a new birth as God's own child. Thank You for forgiving my sin. Help me to live as God's child, sharing the story of Your love with everyone I meet. Amen.

Jesus and the Samaritan Woman

John 4:1–45

What would you do if a new child came to school who was really different from everyone else?

Jesus did most of His teaching in the land called Galilee. But when there were big festivals like Passover, Jesus led His disciples south from Galilee down to the temple, in the land called Judea. But between Galilee and Judea was a land called Samaria. The people who lived there were called Samaritans.

The Jews hated the Samaritans very much, but Jesus didn't. One day when He was traveling through Samaria with His disciples, they entered a Samaritan village around noon. Jesus and His disciples were tired, hungry, and thirsty. So He sent them off to buy food while He sat down by the well to rest.

When a Samaritan woman came to the well, Jesus said, "Give Me a drink."

She looked at Him in surprise and asked why He would want water from her, since Jews hated Samaritans.

Jesus said He would give her living water if she asked Him. Pointing to the well, He said, "Everyone who drinks of this water will be thirsty again, but whoever drinks of the water that I will give him will never be thirsty again." Jesus was teaching her about faith, but she thought He meant actual water. She asked Him to give her that water so she could stop coming to the well.

Jesus said, "Go, call your husband, and come here." The woman answered, "I have no husband." Jesus already knew that. He said, "You are right in saying, 'I have no husband'; for you have had five husbands, and the one you now have is not your husband. What you have said is true."

The woman was amazed Jesus knew all about her. He had never met her before. She told Him she thought He was a prophet. She talked with Jesus about the difference between the ways Jews and Samaritans worshiped God. Jesus told her those differences didn't really matter at all to God. God is a spirit who cares more about faith in our hearts than where we worship Him. She mentioned one thing that both Jews and Samaritans had in common—both groups believed that God's promised Savior was coming, and both were looking forward to meeting Him.

Jesus told her, "I am He."

The woman believed. She was so excited she ran off and told her neighbors, "Come, see a man who told me all that I ever did. Can this be the Christ?"

Many Samaritans heard what she said, and they believed in Jesus. They came and asked Jesus to stay with them. When He stayed and talked with them two extra days, many more Samaritans believed in Him.

Sometimes, it's scary to meet someone who is different from us. But maybe you can think how scary it is to be in a new place where you don't know anyone! This is a great time to be a good friend and tell others all about Jesus' love and forgiveness.

LET'S PRAY: Lord Jesus, thank You for showing me the way to talk to someone who is different from me. Fill my heart with love for all people—especially those who need to hear about Your love. Amen.

Jesus Heals a Man Who Can't Walk

John 5:1–17

Have you ever met someone who couldn't walk? What are some things you couldn't do anymore if you couldn't walk?

The Bible tells us that Jesus healed people who were blind or deaf or had leprosy. In this reading, Jesus healed a man who was not able to walk. It happened in Jerusalem.

This man was lying by a pool called Bethesda (buh-THEZ-duh). He was with a large group of people who were blind, lame, or paralyzed. Since these people couldn't see or move around well, they weren't able to work or hold jobs. So they gathered here by this pool.

They were here because they had heard stories that God sent an angel to this pool from time to time. When the water got stirred up, everyone made their way to the water as fast as they could go, and whoever was the first person to get into the water was supposed to be healed.

Jesus came through the courtyard and saw this man. He knew that he had been there a long, long time. Jesus asked him, "Do you want to be healed?"

The man answered, "Sir, I have no one to put me into the pool when the water is stirred up, and while I am going another steps down before me."

Jesus told him, "Get up, take your bed, and walk." And by the power of His words, Jesus healed the man right away. He got up on his feet, picked up his bed, and started walking. Some Jews saw the man carrying his bed, and they asked him why he was breaking the rules, carrying a load on the Sabbath Day.

The man answered, "The man who healed me, that man said to me, 'Take up your bed, and walk.'" They asked who healed him, but he didn't know. Jesus had disappeared into the crowds.

A little later that day, Jesus found the man in the temple and told him, "See, you are well! Sin no more, that nothing worse may happen to you."

The man went away and told the Jews that Jesus was the man who had healed him and told him to carry his bed. That made some of the Jewish leaders really mad at Jesus. They thought He was breaking the Sabbath rules by working all these miracles. They tried to argue with Him and treat Him in a very mean way.

Jesus told them that God His Father always takes care of His children, and Jesus does too.

This made the Jews even more angry. Jesus wasn't just breaking their Sabbath rules. When He called God His own Father, He was making Himself equal to God. They clearly understood that Jesus was claiming to be God's Son, but they didn't want to believe that to be true.

Jesus did such tremendous things to help people who were hurting—like this man who couldn't walk. Healing this man was another sign that showed that Jesus is the Christ, and people should believe in Him to have a new life.

LET'S PRAY: Lord Jesus, thank You for healing the man so he could get up and walk. Keep me strong in faith so no sin will keep me from You. Amen.

The Good Shepherd

What is your favorite animal? What do you like about it?

Long ago, David wrote beautiful Psalm 23, where he compared himself to a sheep. For many years, he had been a shepherd keeping watch over the sheep of his father, Jesse. He realized God watches over us like a shepherd. So he started writing, "The LORD is my shepherd" (Psalm 23:1). In the tenth chapter of John, Jesus said, "I am the good shepherd."

To understand what Jesus was saying, we need to know a little bit about sheep. Sheep are not strong animals. They are not extra fast, and they don't have a lot of ways to defend themselves. If a wolf attacks a herd of unprotected sheep, it has an easy time grabbing one. Also, sheep easily wander off from one another in search of food to eat. It is easy for them to get lost and hurt.

So a shepherd has a very important job. He has to watch his sheep carefully and always be ready to keep them safe, remembering that many wild animals are hunting after them.

When Jesus said, "I am the good shepherd," He was reminding us of how much we need Him. Like sheep and lambs, we can't see the wolves that are hiding in the tall grass, sneaking up to grab us. The devil, the sinful people around us, and our own sinful desires put us in great danger. But Jesus knows they are there. He is keeping watch over them—and using His Bible and His gifts to protect us from them.

When David offered to fight the giant Goliath, King Saul wasn't sure. David was a young man and Goliath a skilled soldier. But David told him about things he had done when he was a shepherd: "When there came a lion, or a bear, and took a lamb from the flock, I went after him and struck him and delivered it out of his mouth. And if he arose against me, I caught him by his beard and struck him and killed him" (1 Samuel 17:34–35).

That is the greatest thing about Jesus, our Good Shepherd. Each of us was trapped, and the devil had us in great danger. But Jesus didn't leave us. He went to the cross to suffer and die to save us. But He didn't stay dead—a dead shepherd can't help the sheep anymore. No, Jesus rose again, so He will always be our Good Shepherd, protecting us and leading us to heaven.

There are many scary things in this world, but we don't have to be afraid, because Jesus is protecting us and guiding us through life. It's nice to know Jesus is always there. But not every boy and girl knows it. Jesus has given us the happy job of telling others that they have someone watching over them. Jesus wants to protect everyone from every harm and danger and lead them home to heaven.

LET'S PRAY: Lord Jesus, thank You for laying down Your life to save me from the devil, sin, and death. Thank You also for rising to life again on the third day. Because You are my living Good Shepherd, I don't ever need to be afraid. Amen.

Jesus Raises Lazarus

How does it feel when someone you love dies?

Jesus had many good friends beyond His twelve disciples. Three of the closest were two sisters and their brother—Mary, Martha, and Lazarus. They lived in a little village outside of Jerusalem called Bethany.

While Jesus was teaching in Galilee, the sisters sent Him a message that Lazarus was very, very sick. But Jesus told His disciples Lazarus's sickness would not end in death, and He stayed in Galilee two more days.

In Bethany, the sisters stayed at Lazarus's side, waiting for Jesus to come. They watched their brother get sicker and sicker, but Jesus never showed up. Finally, Lazarus died.

On the third day, Jesus told His disciples, "Let us go to Judea again. Our friend Lazarus has fallen asleep, but I go to awaken him." The disciples said, "Lord, if he has fallen asleep, he will recover." Jesus answered, "Lazarus has died, and for your sake I am glad that I was not there, so that you may believe. But let us go to him."

After Lazarus had been buried four days, Martha heard Jesus was coming. She met Him and said, "Lord, if You had been here my brother would not have died. But even now I know that whatever You ask from God, God will give You."

Jesus told her, "Your brother will rise again." Martha said, "I know that he will rise again in the resurrection on the last day." But Jesus answered, "I am the resurrection and the life." He explained that if a person believes in Him, that person will live, even though his or her body may die. And everyone who lives and believes in Him will never suffer the death of their soul in hell. They will instead experience joy and peace in God's presence.

Martha went in and told her sister Mary,

"The Teacher is here and is calling for you." Mary came out, but she was so upset all she could say was, "Lord, if You had been here, my brother would not have died."

Jesus asked where Lazarus's tomb was, and they said, "Lord, come and see." And Jesus cried.

He followed them to the tomb; then, He told them to roll away the stone. After praying to His Father, Jesus called out in a loud voice, "Lazarus, come out!" The dead man came out, all wrapped in cloth. Jesus told them to untie him and let him go.

After Jesus died on the cross, He was wrapped in cloths and laid in a tomb with a big stone rolled in front of it. On the third day, the angel came down and rolled the stone away from the empty tomb to show Jesus had risen from the dead.

If you have had to bury someone you love, you know the pain Martha and Mary felt. But Jesus is the resurrection and the life. He will return on Judgment Day to raise the people we love who died believing in Him. Then, we will live together with them in God's heavenly home forever.

LET'S PRAY: Lord Jesus, thank You for showing Your power over death by raising Lazarus—but first showing us by Your tears how much You care about us and the hurts we feel. Give me such faith in Your resurrection that I may always find joy and hope, even when someone I love very much dies. Amen.

The Transfiguration

What is the most amazing thing you have ever seen?

Peter, James, and John saw Jesus do some amazing things—like healing sick people and walking on water. But on one special night, they saw something even more amazing.

Jesus and these three disciples climbed up a high mountain together. Near the top, Jesus began to pray while the three fell asleep (see Luke 9:32). Suddenly, a bright light startled them. But it was not the moon or the sun—it was Jesus! His face was shining brighter than the sun! His body was shining so brightly it made the clothes He was wearing look dazzling white—like snow on a sunny day that is so bright it makes you squint your eyes.

Peter, James, and John had trouble waking up, but they knew Jesus wasn't alone. Moses and Elijah were standing with Him, and they were shining too! The Old Testament men were talking about Jesus' exodus—something He would do at Jerusalem.

The three disciples didn't understand yet, but Moses and Elijah were talking about how Jesus would die on the cross outside Jerusalem. He would be the Passover Lamb, whose blood is placed on us in our Baptism, so the angel of death will pass over us. Like Moses led the people of Israel out of slavery in Egypt, Jesus will bring us out of slavery to sin and hell and lead us to our promised home in heaven.

At that point, the disciples were wide awake. They saw Moses and Elijah turning to leave. Peter wanted them to stay, so he said, "Lord, it is good that we are here. If You wish, I will make three tents here, one for You and one for Moses and one for Elijah." While Peter was talking, a bright cloud came down and covered them. From the cloud, they heard a voice say, "This is My beloved Son, with whom I am well pleased; listen to Him."

The three disciples were terribly frightened. They fell down on their faces and didn't move until Jesus bent down and touched them. He said, "Rise, and have no fear." They looked up and saw no one was there except Jesus—and He wasn't shining anymore. He looked just the same as before.

As Jesus led them back down the mountain, He told them not to tell anyone else what they had seen. Not until He would rise from the dead.

We call this event Jesus' transfiguration (trans-fig-yur-AY-shuhn). This word talks about something that morphs or changes. With their own eyes, Peter, James, and John saw that Jesus is not only human, but He is also God's almighty Son.

One day, you and I will see Jesus shining in this same beautiful glory forever and ever. Like Moses and Elijah, we will be able to talk with Him and thank Him for saving us. But then that amazing sight will never end—we will be able to see Jesus in all His beautiful brightness and dazzling light forever and ever.

LET'S PRAY: Lord Jesus, I can't wait to see You shining in glory with my own eyes. Until then, help me share Your story with all my family and friends, so they can live with You and see Your glory too. Amen.

Jesus Blesses the Little Children

Matthew 19:13–15

What are some things grown-ups have done that made you feel special?

Jesus loved people very much. He healed those who were sick; He ate and drank with tax collectors and sinners nobody else loved; and He forgave people who felt really bad about things they shouldn't have done. But Jesus also showed His love for another group—little children like you.

Not everyone loves to have children around. Some grown-ups think children are too noisy, too silly, and too much trouble.

Jesus' disciples got upset when they saw parents bringing their little children to Jesus. These moms and dads wanted Jesus to touch their boys and girls and bless them. But the disciples wouldn't let them see Jesus. They sent them away.

Jesus was not happy when He saw this. He told His disciples to let the little children come to Him and not to stand in their way. He told them that God's kingdom belonged to little children. In fact, they would not even see heaven unless they received God's kingdom the way little children do (see Mark 10:15).

What did He mean? Grown-ups work hard to earn money to pay for houses, cars, clothes, and food for their children. Sometimes, all that work makes grown-ups think they are doing it all, and they forget that really God is the Father taking care of them and their families. They think it is all up to them—if they don't make the money, their families won't have all the things they need.

Little children are not like that. They don't worry about where their food and clothes will come from. They trust their mom and dad to give it to them. That is how children help grown-ups in the Church.

When it comes to getting to heaven, children just like you remind us we are all little children who can't do it ourselves. That is why our Father in heaven sent His Son, Jesus, to save us. Jesus lived on earth, carefully keeping all His Father's commands, and He died on the cross to pay for all the bad things we do. When He baptized us, God adopted us as His own children and opened heaven for us. We don't have to worry about food, clothes, a house, or anything that our families need—because God our Father promises He will take care of us.

Jesus' disciples stopped sending the parents and their children away. As they came near, they saw Jesus had a huge smile on His face as He spread His arms wide for the little children. He held them tight, put His hands on them, and blessed them.

As you grow up, don't forget how wonderful it feels to learn about God's love for you. You have a special place in Jesus' heart and a special place in His family. And before you grow up, please pray for God to help you remind your mom and dad, your grandparents, and all the grown-ups at church just how much they can trust Jesus.

LET'S PRAY: Lord Jesus, I am so happy that You care about little children like me. Give me Your Holy Spirit, so I can love Your Bible and always trust You like I trust You today. Amen.

Jesus and Zacchaeus

Luke 19:1–10

When was the last time you wanted to see something but were too short to see it?

Do you ever find it hard being young? When your feet don't reach the floor as you sit in a big chair? When you want to see an animal at the zoo, but can't see past the grown-ups standing in front of you?

Now imagine you are all grown up—but you are still small like you are today. You can't see when you are in a crowd of people. That's how it was for a tax collector named Zacchaeus (za-KEE-uhs). He lived in Jericho, and he learned that Jesus was passing through town on His way to the Passover in Jerusalem. Zacchaeus was a chief tax collector—in charge of all the tax collectors in the area. So the Jewish people hated him even more than they hated most tax collectors.

But Zacchaeus had heard things about Jesus. He heard Jesus talked to tax collectors and ate with them. Jesus even chose one named Matthew to be one of His twelve disciples. So when Zacchaeus heard Jesus was passing through town, he wanted to get a look at Him. But he was too short to see Jesus over the crowds. So he ran ahead and climbed up into a tree.

And sure enough, from the tree, Zacchaeus could see the big crowd of people coming through town. And in the middle of that crowd, he saw Jesus, coming closer and closer. Suddenly, Jesus came near his tree, stopped, and looked right up at him. With a big smile, Jesus said, "Zacchaeus, hurry and come down, for I must stay at your house today."

Zacchaeus was so happy that he rushed down, led Jesus to his house, and made a big feast for Him. As he talked with Jesus, he thought about the way he had treated the people he collected taxes from. He felt bad because he took more money than he should have.

He turned to Jesus and made a promise: "Behold, Lord, half of my goods I give to the poor. And if I have defrauded anyone of anything, I restore it fourfold." That meant if he took more money than he should have, he would pay back four times that amount.

Jesus replied, "Today salvation has come to this house, since he also is a son of Abraham. For I came to seek and to save the lost."

Imagine Jesus coming into your church. Everyone crowds around Him and you are trying to get a look, but you are too short to see. Suddenly, you hear Jesus telling everyone to step back because He has come to sit and talk with you. That's what He did when He baptized you. It is what He does every time you open this Bible and listen to His words. He sits beside you and talks with you. What a wonderful Savior we have!

LET'S PRAY: Lord Jesus, Zacchaeus was so happy when You told him to come down so You could go and spend the day with him. Thank You for coming to me in my Baptism and for talking to me when I read my Bible. Make me as excited as Zacchaeus to tell Your story to boys and girls who do not know You. Amen.

The Triumphal Entry Matthew 21:1–11

What is your favorite holiday? What makes it so special?

Every year in spring, the Jews gathered together in Jerusalem to celebrate the Passover feast. It was a time as happy and exciting for them as Christmas is for us. At Passover, the Jews remembered how God raised up Moses and used ten plagues to bring His people Israel out of slavery in Egypt. The people spread the blood of the Passover lamb on their doors, and when the angel saw the blood he passed over their houses, saving their firstborn.

Huge crowds came up the road to Jerusalem, and Jesus joined them just as He did many Passovers before. But this time, Jesus rode on a donkey. That's a work animal Jewish kings like King David rode into town. Roman kings and emperors rode on horses. The horse reminded the people of their king's power. But the donkey reminded the Jews that their King was coming to serve them, protect them, and take care of them.

The crowds around Jesus were very excited. They had traveled with Him, listened to His wonderful teachings, and seen the healing miracles He worked. They started singing and shouting many things to Jesus.

"Hosanna to the Son of David!" *Hosanna* means "save us now." They believed Jesus was the promised Savior, the Christ or Messiah. They asked Him to save them.

"Blessed is He who comes in the name of the Lord!" They said Jesus was happy to be coming on God's mission.

"Hosanna in the highest!" They shouted for God to save them through Jesus.

And they were right—that was exactly what Jesus was riding into Jerusalem to do for us. This Sunday started the most important week of all. On Sunday, Jesus rode into Jerusalem to save us from our sins. On Friday, He was punished on the cross for our sins, and He died in our place. Then on the following Sunday, He rose from the dead.

Sadly, many of the Jews traveling with Him did not yet understand this. They thought He had come to be an earthly king who would set Israel free and drive out the Romans. But Jesus came to save us from a bigger enemy than the Roman emperor. He came to save us from Satan and being separated forever from God in hell.

Next time you go to church and there is Communion, notice the song we sing when we get ready for Communion. We sing many of the same words these crowds were singing and shouting to Jesus. The reason we do this is because we are celebrating that Jesus is coming to us again—to give us His body and blood with the bread and wine of Communion. In a few years, you will be receiving His body and blood for yourself. But as you wait for that great day, be sure to sing this song with joy because Jesus is coming.

LET'S PRAY: Lord Jesus, it was a great day when You rode the donkey into Jerusalem. You came to save us from our sins. Thank You for coming to us in so many ways now—in Baptism, in Your Bible, and in Holy Communion. Amen.

Jesus Clears the Temple

Mark 11:15–19

Can you think of a time when it would be okay to be angry with someone?

Jesus rode a donkey into Jerusalem on the Sunday before He died on the cross. Large crowds of people welcomed Him; they shouted and sang. But not everyone was happy to see Jesus ride into Jerusalem. The chief priests and Jewish leaders didn't believe in Jesus, and it made them really mad to hear people singing and shouting to Him that He was the great Savior God had promised to Adam and Eve. These leaders wanted to find a way to get rid of Jesus, but they were afraid the crowds would turn against them.

Jesus went up to the temple grounds to teach. When He entered the temple, He got really, really angry. He saw tables set up for people to buy animals they needed for their sacrifices. There were birdcages with pigeons and doves. There were sheep and lambs, goats and bulls. The animals were noisy, and the people buying and selling them had to shout to be heard over that noise.

Jesus knew people needed to buy animals for their sacrifices, so that wasn't what made Him mad. He was upset that they were doing this in the temple! These should have been sold in the market a short way across town. People came to the temple to worship God, hear His Word, and pray. But how could they hear and pray when there was so much noise from the animals, the people shouting, and the coins clinking on the tables?

Jesus suddenly ran up to the tables and flipped them upside down. The coins went flying everywhere! He knocked over the chairs the people were sitting on to sell the birds. He made a whip out of cords and drove away the animals and the people who were buying and selling (John 2:15). He told them, "It is written,

'My house will be called a house of prayer,' but you have made it a den of robbers."

Worship and prayer are very important to Jesus. They should be important to you and me too. God comes to us when we pray and read His Word, when we sing together in church. That is why our parents tell us to be quiet in church—so that we will pay attention to what God is saying to us, and so the people sitting around us will be able to listen to the pastor teach and preach.

That is also why we fold our hands, close our eyes, and bow our heads when we pray. Hands that are folded together won't reach for things that will take our attention away from God. Eyes that are closed won't be looking for things to think about instead of what is being prayed. Heads that are bowed make it a little harder to hear strange noises and voices that make us try to figure out where they are coming from.

This is what being in God's house is all about, why we listen and pray—so God can come to us, speak to us, and remind us just how much He loves us.

LET'S PRAY: Lord Jesus, thank You for clearing out the temple court so the people You love could hear what You wanted to tell them. Clear my mind when I read Your Bible, when I pray, and when I am in church and Sunday School, so I can listen to Your wonderful promises. Amen.

What do you think it would have been like to eat supper with Jesus?

On Friday, Jesus would die on the cross. But on Thursday night, He gathered with His twelve disciples for one last meal together—the Passover. He wanted to show them how much He loved them, and He wanted to make them ready for the terrible things they would soon see.

But first, Jesus got up from the table and took off His outer clothes (like we would take off a jacket). He wrapped a towel around His waist, got down on His hands and knees, and washed His disciples' feet. He taught us that no job is too low or dirty when we can show people how much we love them. When He was done, He sat back down and they started eating (see John 13:1–11).

Then Jesus felt really sad and upset. He knew one of His twelve disciples did not love Him like before and was planning to do something bad. Jesus knew Judas had been paid money from the Jewish leaders who hated Jesus. Judas promised to tell them when they could arrest Jesus without the big crowds around. Jesus loved Judas as a brother—but Judas was treating Him like an enemy.

Jesus told the twelve disciples, "One of you will betray Me." The disciples were upset. Looking at one another, each one asked Jesus, "Is it I?" Jesus answered, "It is he to whom I will give this morsel of bread when I have dipped it" (John 13:26). He dipped it in a bowl and then gave it to Judas and said, "What you are going to do, do quickly" (John 13:27). Right away, Judas went out into the darkness of night. None of the other disciples realized what Judas was going to do.

Later, Jesus took some bread, said a prayer of thanks for it, broke it, and gave it to His disciples. He said, "Take, eat; this is My body." Then after supper, Jesus took a cup of wine. He said a prayer of thanks, then gave it to His disciples and said, "Drink of it, all of you, for this is My blood of the covenant, which is poured out for many for the forgiveness of sins."

Then Jesus told His disciples that during that same night all of them would run away from Him. Peter answered, "Though they all fall away because of You, I will never fall away." Jesus told him, "Truly, I tell you, this very night, before the rooster crows, you will deny Me three times." Peter said, "Even if I must die with You, I will not deny You!"

Can you imagine what it would have been like to be in that Upper Room and have Jesus get down on His hands and knees to wash your feet? When you were baptized, Jesus did something like that. He was right there with you, washing away all of your sins. When you get older, you will be able to receive Holy Communion. Jesus will come to you again in the bread and wine, giving you His very own body and blood, which took away your sins on the cross.

LET'S PRAY: Lord Jesus, You loved me and washed away all my sins. Help me show my love to my family and my friends, too, and tell them about Your love. Amen.

Jesus Prays in the Garden

Tell about a time you had to do something you really didn't want to do.

After the Last Supper, Jesus led His disciples up the Mount of Olives to a place called the Garden of Gethsemane (geth-SEM-uh-nee). Leaving eight disciples behind, He took Peter, James, and John along with Him. He told them to watch with Him and pray, and then He walked on about as far as you can throw a stone. Then He knelt down and prayed.

Doesn't it seem like praying should be really easy? There in the garden, Jesus showed us it can be very, very hard sometimes. He loved His Father, and He wanted to do what His Father sent Him to do. He wanted to save us, but it hurt Him to think about what would happen on that cross. It wasn't just that the nails would really, really hurt. It wasn't just that His friends would all leave Him and He would be surrounded by people making fun of Him. What really hurt was knowing God His Father would turn against Him and punish Him for all our sins.

Jesus was crying when He prayed, "Father, if You are willing, remove this cup from Me. Nevertheless, not My will, but Yours, be done." No matter what, Jesus wanted to do what His heavenly Father wanted, and He wanted to save us from our sins. But He asked if there was any other way than the cross. Knowing there wasn't, He prayed, "Not My will, but Yours, be done."

God the Father saw how much His Son was hurting. So He sent an angel to strengthen Jesus. After that, Jesus prayed even harder. He prayed so hard He was sweating, and blood mixed in with that sweat.

Jesus prayed for nearly an hour; then, He went to check on Peter, James, and John. They were all sleeping. Jesus woke them up and reminded them to pray.

Jesus went away and started praying again. He said the same thing this second time: "My Father, if this cannot pass unless I drink it, Your will be done" (Matthew 26:42). After another hour of praying, Jesus checked in on the three disciples again. But they were still sleeping.

One more time, Jesus returned to pray. After another hour, praying the same words again, Jesus was finally ready to go to the cross and save us from sin and hell.

He woke up His disciples and told them it was time to go; Judas was coming.

Sometimes, praying is a very, very hard thing to do, like when we have to face a bully, take a test, give a report, go to a doctor or the dentist, have surgery, or move away from all our friends. These are the times it is hard to pray Jesus' words "Not what I want, but what You want, God!"

But Jesus promises to be right there with you when you pray. And at the end, that problem will pass away, just as Jesus' hours on the cross finally came to an end.

LET'S PRAY: Lord Jesus, thank You for praying so You were ready to go to the cross for all of us. Give me courage and strength to pray in hard times so I'll be ready to do what You want too! Amen.

What would you do if someone did something really, really mean to you?

After the Last Supper, Jesus went out to pray in the Garden of Gethsemane. When He was finished, He woke up His disciples and watched a crowd coming toward the garden. They were carrying torches, clubs, and swords. In front was one of the Twelve—Judas.

After all that time praying, Jesus was ready. He stepped forward, past the other disciples, to meet Judas and the soldiers as they came near.

Judas walked up to Jesus and kissed Him so the crowd would know whom to arrest. Jesus asked, "Judas, would you betray the Son of Man with a kiss?" (Luke 22:48).

Judas didn't realize what a terrible thing he was doing—but Jesus knew that later, when Judas saw that Jesus would be put to death on the cross, he would feel really, really guilty. If only Judas would remember how much Jesus loved him. If only he would wait until the third day when Jesus rose from the dead! Then, Jesus could have appeared to him, forgiven him, and given him back his place among the Twelve.

Jesus turned from Judas to the soldiers and asked whom they were looking for. They answered, "Jesus of Nazareth." With the powerful voice of the Son of God, Jesus answered, "I am He." His words were so powerful they pushed the crowd backward and made them fall to the ground. Judas fell down with them.

When they got back up, Jesus again asked whom they were looking for. For a second time, they answered, "Jesus of Nazareth." Jesus said, "I told you that I am He. So, if you seek Me, let these men go." And with that, Jesus let His eleven disciples run away to safety. But Peter didn't realize Jesus was in control. He grabbed a sword, ran up to the soldiers, and swung it down with all his might. It cut off the ear of the high priest's servant.

Before the soldiers could strike back, Jesus stepped forward, turned to Peter and said, "Put your sword away. Shall I not drink the cup that the Father has given Me?" He walked to the wounded man, touched his ear, and healed him (see Luke 22:51). The eleven disciples scattered, and the guards and soldiers tied Jesus up and led Him back into Jerusalem.

As Jesus found with Judas, it hurts really, really badly when someone you love, someone you trust, does something bad to you. We want to be angry with that person forever, to never, ever be his or her friend again. But Jesus warns us not to hold onto that kind of anger. It may feel good for a little while, but God wants us to keep loving and forgiving others the way Jesus kept loving Judas and keeps loving and forgiving each of us.

LET'S PRAY: Jesus, it hurt You really badly when Judas betrayed You. But You still loved him and wanted to forgive him. Teach me how to stay away from sins like Judas's, but when I do sin, help me realize what I have done and turn to You to ask Your forgiveness. Then, I can live in peace and joy as I tell others about Your wonderful love. Amen.

Jesus' Jewish Trial

How does it feel to be blamed for doing something you didn't do?

Jesus left the Last Supper and then went to pray. There in the garden, He was arrested, and the guards and soldiers led Him to the house of the high priest Caiaphas (KAY-uh-fuhs). All the Jewish judges were gathered for Jesus' trial. In a trial, a person is accused of doing something bad. Judges listen to witnesses who saw or heard what happened, and then they decide if the person did it or not.

So Jesus was on trial, but it wasn't going to be a fair trial. Jesus hadn't done anything wrong, but the judges wanted to put Him to death anyway. They were angry because Jesus said things that showed the people they were sinners who needed forgiveness. They were also afraid the crowds would make Him a king and the Romans would come in and destroy the temple.

But as Caiaphas the high priest started the trial, he was having a hard time. Way back in Moses' time, God gave Israel a rule that said two witnesses had to agree before someone could be punished for doing something wrong—one witness was not enough. And the high priest couldn't find two witnesses who said the same thing. Even when the high priest looked for witnesses to lie about Jesus, he still couldn't find two stories that matched.

The high priest finally turned to Jesus. He said, "Tell us if You are the Christ, the Son of God." Jesus answered, "You have said so." He meant everything the high priest said was true—Jesus was and is the Christ, the Son of God. But Jesus didn't stop there. He warned the Jewish leaders that they would all see Him sitting at God the Father's right hand and coming on the clouds of heaven to be their judge on Judgment Day.

That was what the high priest was hoping to hear. Now he could accuse Jesus of claiming to be God—which would be a terrible thing for Jesus to say if it were not true. But it was true and always will be true. The high priest asked the Jewish court what they had decided. They said Jesus should die on the cross for saying He was God's Son.

Even though they wanted Jesus to die, they couldn't put Jesus to death on the cross. Only Pontius Pilate (PON-shuhs PIGH-luht), the Roman governor, could do that. But it was the middle of the night, and they had to wait until the sun came up to take Jesus to Pilate. So the leaders took turns hitting Jesus, slapping Him in the face, and spitting on Him. They covered His eyes with a blindfold and then hit Him in the face and demanded that He tell them who had struck Him.

Jesus stood silently and let Himself get beaten up. Why? Because that is what you and I and all of us deserve for all the bad things we do to one another—and for not doing the good things we should do. In this trial, we see Jesus already carrying our sins and suffering in our place so we will never have to.

LET'S PRAY: Jesus, You were hurt by the people You loved and were ready to go to the cross to save. Forgive me for the times I don't do what You say and treat other people badly. Amen.

Peter Denies Jesus

Have you ever had the chance to speak up for someone who was being treated badly, but you kept quiet? What kept you from helping that person?

After Jesus was arrested in the garden, He was taken to the high priest's house. While He was inside being questioned, Peter was sitting with the guards in the high priest's courtyard. He wanted to find out what was happening to Jesus. At first, he seemed very brave to be there, but soon Peter wished he had run away like the other disciples.

It all started when a servant girl walked up to Peter and said, "You also were with the Nazarene, Jesus."

Peter was scared of the guards and soldiers and what they would do to him, so he said, "I neither know nor understand what you mean." That was Peter's first denial.

Peter was scared to stay there with the guards, so he walked toward the gateway. As he did, a rooster crowed.

But the servant girl again told the bystanders, "This man is one of them."

He lied and for the second time denied knowing Jesus.

The guards were quiet for a little bit, but before long they gathered around him again. They had listened carefully to what Peter had said—and how he had said it. They noticed Peter didn't talk like they did; he was from the north, and they were from the south.

They said, "Certainly you, too, are one of them, for you are a Galilean."

Peter knew he was in big trouble; no one was believing him. So he swore, which means he asked God to listen to what he said and punish him if he was lying. And he called down a curse on himself, something like, "If I know this Jesus, may God strike me dead!"

Clearly Peter wasn't thinking about God—he was just looking for some way to save himself from the guards and what they might do to him. He should have thought about what Jesus once taught him: "Do not fear those who kill the body but cannot kill the soul. Rather fear Him who can destroy both soul and body in hell" (Matthew 10:28).

But Peter wasn't thinking about Judgment Day, or of how God could punish him in hell. All he could think of was how to get out of there alive. He said, "I do not know this man of whom you speak."

And while he was still saying his third denial, Peter heard the rooster crow again. He remembered how Jesus had told him at the Last Supper, "Before the rooster crows twice, you will deny Me three times." Then Peter went outside the courtyard and started crying very hard.

As Peter learned, it is hard to speak up for a person when everyone else in the crowd is attacking that person. But that is exactly what Jesus did when He was dying on the cross. He prayed, "Father, forgive them, for they know not what they do" (Luke 23:34). Now, He gives you courage and strength to share the Good News of His death and resurrection.

LET'S PRAY: Lord Jesus, You felt the sting of Peter's denials. Forgive me the times I stay quiet when You want me to speak up. Give me courage to tell everyone I meet about Your love. Amen.

Jesus before Pontius Pilate

John 18:28–19:16

What would you do if a bunch of kids wanted you to do something that was wrong?

After He was arrested, Jesus was led to the Jewish leaders, who decided He must die. But the Romans would not let them put a person to death. Only the Roman governor, Pontius Pilate (PON-shuhs PIGH-luht), could do that. Early Friday morning, they brought Jesus before him.

Pilate asked what Jesus had done wrong.

The Jewish leaders told Pilate that Jesus had broken three laws: "We found this man misleading our nation and forbidding us to give tribute to Caesar, and saying that He Himself is Christ, a king" (Luke 23:2). Pilate went into his headquarters and asked Jesus, "Are You the King of the Jews?"

Jesus answered, "My kingdom is not of this world. If My kingdom were of this world, My servants would have been fighting, that I might not be delivered over to the Jews. But My kingdom is not from the world."

Pilate answered, "So You are a king?"

Jesus answered, "You say that I am a king. I have come into the world to bear witness to the truth. Everyone who is of the truth listens to My voice."

Pilate told the Jews, "I find no guilt in Him." But instead of setting Jesus free, he thought he could make the Jews ask him to set Jesus free. He said, "You have a custom that I should release one man for you at the Passover." He asked them to choose between Jesus and Barabbas (buh-RAB-uhs), a really bad man who had killed some people. The Jewish leaders convinced the crowds to call for Barabbas to be set free and for Jesus to be crucified.

Pilate was surprised. He knew Jesus had done nothing wrong, but he thought if he had Jesus whipped that would satisfy the leaders who hated Jesus so much.

So the Roman soldiers took Jesus and whipped Him really badly. They made a crown out of thorns and put it on His head. They put a purple robe on Him and kneeled in front of Him, saying, "Hail, King of the Jews!"

Pilate brought Jesus out to the Jews and said, "Behold the man!" He hoped the Jews would think Jesus had already suffered enough. But when they saw Him, they shouted, "Crucify Him, crucify Him!"

Finally, Pilate gave up. He took a bowl and washed his hands in front of them all, and said, "I am innocent of this man's blood" (Matthew 27:24). He set Barabbas free and ordered his soldiers to take Jesus outside the city and crucify Him.

When people bigger or more powerful than us threaten us because of our faith in Jesus, we know what we should say, but we are afraid. We are afraid of what people will think or say or do to us if we speak of Jesus being our hope and Savior. The Holy Spirit promises to be with us to make us bold and strong so we can speak of Jesus when no one else will. When we fail, we can tell God we are sorry and know that Jesus suffered and died to take away all our sin and that the Holy Spirit empowers us.

LET'S PRAY: Lord Jesus, You told Pilate about the kingdom of heaven because You wanted him to believe and be saved. Give me and all Christians courage to speak up for You and to defend one another so the world will know You love them too. Amen.

The Crucifixion and Jesus' Last Words

John 19:1–30

Why did Jesus die on the cross?

The Roman soldiers made Jesus carry His cross through Jerusalem to a hill called Golgotha outside the city. There, they nailed His hands and feet to the cross and raised Him up between two criminals (see Mark 15:27). They put a sign over His head that read, "Jesus of Nazareth, the King of the Jews."

Jesus prayed, "Father, forgive them, for they know not what they do" (Luke 23:34). He was praying for the Roman soldiers, but also for Judas and Peter, Caiaphas the high priest and the Jewish court, Pontius Pilate, the criminals who were making fun of Him, the crowds who were watching, and for you, me, and all people, because He was being punished for all our sins.

At first, both criminals made fun of Jesus (see Matthew 27:44). But then, one changed his mind. He asked the other, "Do you not fear God?" (Luke 23:40). He knew he would stand before God to be judged after he died. He told the other they both had done very bad things and deserved to die on a cross. But Jesus had done nothing wrong. In the faith given to him by the Holy Spirit, he prayed, "Jesus, remember me when You come into Your kingdom" (v. 42). Jesus said, "Truly, I say to you, today you will be with Me in paradise" (v. 43).

Jesus looked out and saw His mother, Mary, and His friend John, one of the twelve disciples. Jesus looked at Mary, nodded His head toward John, and said, "Woman, behold your son!" Then, He looked at John, nodded toward Mary, and said, "Behold, your mother!" From that hour, John took Mary into his home and took care of her.

At noon, the sun stopped shining and it grew very dark (see Luke 23:44). Jesus was being punished in our place for our sins. God the Father left Jesus all alone to suffer the punishment for all our sins. This went on for three long hours until Jesus cried out, "My God, My God, why have You forsaken Me?" (Matthew 27:46).

When Jesus knew all our sins were paid in full, He said, "I thirst." The soldiers gave Him some sour wine to drink.

After drinking, Jesus shouted in a loud voice, "It is finished." He had finished everything God the Father had sent Him to do. The serpent's head was crushed (see Genesis 3:15). Every sin had been paid for, and heaven now stood open for everyone who believes in Jesus.

Finally, Jesus prayed, "Father, into Your hands I commit My spirit" (Luke 23:46). Then, He died.

Many people are scared to die. But we don't have to be. Jesus went there first. He died, was buried, and rose to life again. Like He promised the criminal who died next to Him, He promises all who believe in Him that when we die, our spirits will leave this world of hurts and sorrows and be with Him in paradise. Then, on the Last Day, He will come back and raise our bodies to everlasting life.

LET'S PRAY: Lord Jesus, whenever I am afraid of dying, remind me of Your death and resurrection. Remind me You will take my spirit home to heaven when I die and raise my body back to life when You come back. Amen.

Jesus Is Buried

Why is it sad when someone dies?

Jesus died on the cross at about 3:00 in the afternoon. The sad women stood by the cross wondering what would happen to His body. They saw two Jewish leaders come up to the crosses. Both were from the Jewish court that decided Jesus should die. But these two did not agree with that decision. They were followers of Jesus who kept their faith secret—until now.

One was Nicodemus, a Jewish leader who once visited Jesus at night (John 3). He believed Jesus was from God and even told the Jewish leaders they should give Jesus a fair chance (John 7:50–51). The second was a man named Joseph from a town called Arimathea (air-ih-muh-THEE-uh). He was a very important Jewish leader. He was a good man who was looking for the promised Savior and believed Jesus was that Savior. But he didn't tell anyone because he was afraid the other Jewish leaders would throw him out of the Jewish court.

After Jesus died, Joseph went to Pontius Pilate and asked him for permission to take Jesus' body down from the cross and bury it. When Pilate learned Jesus was dead, he gave Joseph permission.

Joseph and Nicodemus took Jesus' body down from the cross. It was late, and they had to hurry before the sun went down and the day of rest started. While they carried Jesus' body to Joseph's own new tomb in a garden nearby, the women followed them.

Joseph and Nicodemus cleaned Jesus' body as best they could and wrapped it in cloth with spices. They laid it in the tomb and then rolled a huge stone over the entrance and walked away. The women paid close attention so they could remember where the tomb was. They went home and planned to buy more spices so when Sunday morning came, they could return and give Jesus' body a more careful, loving burial.

Meanwhile on Saturday morning, the chief priests remembered something Jesus said before He died. He said He would be killed and rise again on the third day. They really didn't believe Jesus would come alive again—they didn't believe there was life after someone died. But they were afraid Jesus' disciples might steal His body from the tomb and start telling people He rose from the dead.

So they went to Pilate and asked for soldiers to guard Jesus' tomb to make sure this wouldn't happen. Pilate gave them soldiers who went and stood watch at the tomb to make sure Jesus' body stayed there.

When we die, our spirits will go to be with Jesus in paradise, just like the robber who died with Him (Luke 23:39–43). We will see Him shining in glory, and we will be very happy and excited. We won't really worry about what will happen to our bodies—God will take care of them. On the Last Day, Jesus will return and raise our bodies to life again.

LET'S PRAY: Lord God, heavenly Father, thank You for sending Joseph and Nicodemus to take care of Jesus' body. Remind us that You will take care of us all through life—and even after we die—until Jesus returns and raises our bodies and makes them perfect and shining in bright glory forever. In Jesus' name. Amen.

Jesus Rises from the Dead

Think of a time when you were really, really sad. Did you ever think you could be happy again?

Many times during the months before Jesus went up to Jerusalem, He told His disciples He was going to suffer and die. And each time, He also told them He would rise again on the third day. But the disciples didn't remember. They all thought He was going to Jerusalem to become king—instead, they saw Him killed on the cross. Their dreams of ruling with Jesus were dead, and they were filled with sadness. They forgot all about His promise to rise again.

On the second day, Saturday, they stayed hidden in Jerusalem because they were afraid they would be captured and killed too. Since that day was a Sabbath, the women rested, waiting for the third day, Sunday, to take spices and give Jesus' body a better burial. They forgot all about His promise to rise from the dead too.

Early Sunday morning, the women started off for the tomb. As they walked along, they remembered the huge stone Joseph and Nicodemus had rolled in front of it. They weren't strong enough to roll it back, so they wondered how they were going to get inside.

Suddenly there was an earthquake, and an angel came down from heaven, rolled the stone back, and sat on it. When the guards saw the angel, they were terrified. They shook and fell down like they were dead. The angel waited for the women.

When the women came, the angel told them, "Do not be afraid, for I know that you are looking for Jesus who was crucified. He is not here, for He has risen, as He said. Come, see the place where He lay."

They looked in and saw that Jesus' body was missing. There was only the cloth and some spices lying where His body had been.

The angel told them, "Go quickly and tell His disciples that He has risen from the dead, and behold, He is going before you to Galilee; there you will see Him."

The women turned and rushed back toward the city to tell Jesus' disciples. But while they were on the way, Jesus met them and said, "Greetings!" They came close, grabbed hold of His feet, and worshiped Him. Jesus told them, "Do not be afraid; go and tell My brothers to go to Galilee, and there they will see Me."

Friday had been the saddest day in these women's lives, but on Sunday morning Jesus turned their sorrow into great joy. Sometimes we have sad days when bad things happen and they leave us hurt. We might think we will never be happy again. But Jesus can take away that hurt. By His death and resurrection, He has given us a bright, new future. Like the women, we have a very good reason to rejoice and be happy!

LET'S PRAY: Lord Jesus, God Your Father raised You from the dead to show You took away our sins and destroyed them on the cross. When bad things happen and I'm scared and sad, fill me with joy and peace, because You are with me to take care of me and lead me to my home in heaven. Amen.

On the Road to Emmaus

Luke 24:13–35

Did you ever hear news so good you felt you were burning inside?

Jesus died on the cross on Friday; He rose from the dead on Sunday. Some of the women went out to the tomb and heard the angels' good news that Jesus had risen; then they saw Jesus and talked with Him.

When the women told the disciples that they had talked with Jesus, the men didn't believe them. Two men were so sad and upset, they left Jerusalem. These two were not part of Jesus' twelve apostles. They were part of a larger group of disciples or believers. One was named Cleopas (KLEE-oh-puhs), but we don't know the name of the other.

They walked along a road that passed through a village called Emmaus (ih-MAY-us). As they walked along, they talked about all the things that had happened. Jesus came near and started walking along with them, but they didn't recognize Him. He asked them, "What are you talking about?"

They stopped walking and looked at Him with sad faces. Cleopas asked Him, "Are You the only visitor to Jerusalem who does not know the things that have happened there?" Jesus answered, "What things?"

The two started telling Jesus about Himself. They said He was a prophet who was mighty in what He said and did. They told how the chief priests and rulers had handed Him over to Pilate and that He had been crucified. They talked about how they had thought Jesus was going to save Israel.

Then they said, "Some women from our company amazed us. They were at the tomb early this morning, and when they didn't find His body, they came back saying they had seen angels who said He was alive."

Jesus said, "O foolish ones, and slow of heart to believe all that the prophets have spoken!" He told them the Messiah had to suffer like this first and then enter His glory by rising from the dead. Then He went through the Old Testament and taught them what God had written about His suffering, death, and resurrection.

By now it was late in the day. The two disciples were stopping in Emmaus for the night, but Jesus acted like He was going to go farther. The two begged Him to stay with them, so He went inside. They sat down for supper, and Jesus took the bread, broke it, said a prayer of thanks, and handed it to them. Suddenly they recognized Jesus—and then He vanished from their sight.

They talked about the wonderful burning feeling they had felt inside when Jesus was walking and talking with them. They were so excited that they ran back to Jerusalem, found Jesus' disciples, and told them how Jesus had walked and talked with them along the road.

Our lives on earth can't always be happy. Bad things happen to us and to the people we love, and those things make us sad. But we don't have to be sad forever. Jesus rose from the dead, and He walks with us every day of our lives. Jesus gives us a joy that no sadness can take away forever.

LET'S PRAY: Heavenly Father, since Jesus died on the cross for my sins, I never have to be afraid You will stop loving me. And because He rose from the dead, I know I will rise again too—and then everything will be perfect forever and ever. Show me someone who needs to hear about Jesus, and give me courage to speak. In Jesus' name. Amen.

Jesus Appears to His Apostles

Think of something really neat that happened at school or with your friends. Now, try to describe it to people from your family who weren't there to see it.

It was the Sunday Jesus rose from the dead. Late in the afternoon, the two men who met Jesus on the road to Emmaus rushed back to Jerusalem. They told the disciples how they had walked and talked with Jesus. The disciples told them that Jesus had appeared to Peter all by himself earlier that afternoon.

While the men were talking about all this exciting news, suddenly Jesus was standing among them, saying, "Peace to you!" Everyone was shocked and scared—they thought they were looking at a ghost because Jesus suddenly appeared, and the door of the house was locked. He asked why they doubted it was really Him. "See My hands and My feet. Touch Me, and see. For a spirit does not have flesh and bones as you see that I have."

There in His hands, they could see the marks from the nails that had held Him to the cross, and they saw the same in His feet. Their shock and fear turned to wonder and amazement. But Jesus wanted them to be sure, so He asked if they had any food left to eat. They gave Him a piece of fish they had broiled, and He ate it in front of them. Now they knew for sure He was not a ghost.

Jesus began to teach them why He had to die on the cross and rise again on the third day. He went through the Old Testament in the Bible and showed them places where God's prophets had told His people bits and pieces of what the Messiah would do when He came to save the world. He opened their minds so they could understand the Old Testament and believe that He was the Messiah who had to "suffer and on the third day rise from the dead."

Jesus told them their work would soon begin. Since they had seen everything Jesus did,

God would send them power from on high, from heaven, and they would start teaching the Jews, the Samaritans, and all the people in the world that we must be sorry for our sins and receive the forgiveness Jesus won when He died for those sins on the cross.

None of us was there to see all that Jesus did to save us from our sins. But the Bible tells us the things Jesus said and did in front of His twelve apostles and many other men and women who saw and heard Him. When we read the Bible, Jesus opens our minds so we can see and hear the same things those people did. Then we are ready to go and tell our friends and neighbors how Jesus came to save us from our sins by dying on the cross and rising to life again on the third day.

Jesus Appears to Thomas

Do you know someone who thinks she knows everything—but she really doesn't?

On the evening of that first Sunday when Jesus rose from the dead, He appeared to His disciples, who were hiding behind locked doors. But Thomas, one of the twelve disciples Jesus chose, wasn't there that night. Later on, when Thomas joined them again, Peter and the other disciples told him over and over again, "We have seen the Lord."

But Thomas thought they were being foolish. He would not let himself believe Jesus was alive unless he saw Him for himself. And even more than that, Thomas insisted that he would have to do more than just look at Jesus to believe He was really alive. He said, "Unless I see in His hands the mark of the nails, and place my finger into the mark of the nails, and place my hand into His side, I will never believe."

Thomas thought the other disciples were foolish, but really he was the one who was being stubborn and silly. He had seen Jesus heal blind, deaf, and paralyzed people; he had seen Jesus walk on water and make storms stop instantly; he had even seen Jesus raise Lazarus from the dead—so why did he refuse to believe Jesus could have risen from the dead?

Jesus could have left Thomas alone in his sad unbelief, but one week later, on the next Sunday night, Jesus made a special visit to the disciples. This time, Thomas was with them. Even though the door was locked, Jesus came and stood among them. He said, "Peace be with you." Then, He turned to Thomas, held out His hands, and said, "Put your finger here, and see My hands; and put out your hand, and place it in My side." He told Thomas to stop refusing to believe, and believe.

Thomas answered, "My Lord and my God!"

Jesus answered, "Have you believed because you have seen Me? Blessed are those who have not seen and yet have believed."

Plenty of people are like Thomas. They refuse to believe anything they can't see and touch. They think we are foolish to believe that God created the world or that He sent a terrible flood from which only Noah's family survived or that Jesus rose from the dead. They think they are smarter than that! That's what Thomas thought—until Jesus appeared to him.

God is so much bigger, stronger, and smarter than any of us will ever be. If He tells us something in His Bible, we can believe it and we should believe it—no matter what people in our world think and no matter how smart they seem to be. People may say you have to be really stupid to believe in Jesus, but remember this: That is how Thomas once felt. He didn't feel that way after he saw Jesus! And like the other disciples, Thomas was so sure Jesus died and rose again that he was willing to die rather than say it wasn't true.

LET'S PRAY: Lord Jesus, thank You for showing Yourself to Thomas so he could stop being so stubborn and know that You are really alive again. Help me trust everything You say. Amen.

237

Jesus Restores Peter

John 21:1–19

Have you ever really hurt a friend and felt so guilty that you were afraid to see him again? What could you do to be sure he still loves you?

few weeks after Jesus rose from the dead, Peter and Jesus' other disciples went back to Galilee. Peter told them, "I am going fishing." Several disciples joined him. They spent all that night fishing but didn't catch even one fish.

Early in the morning, a man on the shore called out to them, "Children, do you have any fish?" They answered no. He said, "Cast the net on the right side of the boat, and you will find some." They did—and the net was so heavy with fish they were not able to haul it into the boat.

Right away, John told Peter, "It is the Lord!" Simon Peter immediately threw himself into the water and swam to shore. The others rowed the boat in because they were not far from shore. When Peter came close to Jesus, he saw a charcoal fire with fish cooking on it. When the disciples arrived, they ate the breakfast Jesus had prepared for them.

After breakfast, Jesus turned to Peter and asked, "Simon, son of John, do you love Me more than these?" Peter was quick to answer, "Yes, Lord; You know that I love You." Jesus told him, "Feed My lambs."

A second time, Jesus asked, "Simon, son of John, do you love Me?" Peter answered, "Yes, Lord; You know that I love You." Jesus answered, "Tend My sheep."

Then, a third time, Jesus asked Peter, "Simon, son of John, do you love Me?" Peter was hurt. Didn't Jesus believe him?

Jesus was making Peter think about the Last Supper, when Jesus had told Peter he would deny Him three times before the rooster crowed. Peter had argued that he would never deny knowing Jesus. But a few hours later, he had denied Him three times as he stood outside with the guards warming himself by the charcoal fire. Three times, Peter had had the chance to show how much he loved Jesus, but each time he had said, "I don't know the man."

Peter could not prove his love—not here by the Sea of Galilee. He didn't try to argue like he did at the Last Supper. All he could do was ask Jesus to look into his heart. He said, "Lord, You know everything; You know that I love You." Jesus answered, "Feed My sheep."

Then, He told Peter what would happen many years later. He told Peter he would get the chance to show his love for Jesus again—and this time the Holy Spirit would make Peter strong to die on a cross, showing his great love for Jesus.

Sometimes, we do bad things that make us feel so awful, like we could never be loved again. But just as Jesus forgave Peter and made him strong to do the work God wanted him to do, Jesus forgives us and makes us strong to love one another and serve God.

LET'S PRAY: Lord Jesus, thank You for making Peter strong again. Make me strong when I am weak, so I can tell others of Your love. Amen.

239

Jesus Ascends into Heaven

Do you have grandparents or family members who live far away? How does it feel when they have to leave after a visit?

For forty days after He rose from the dead, Jesus showed Himself to His disciples in many different places and times. There was no doubt that He had died but was alive again.

One of the last times He showed Himself was on a mountain in Galilee. A large number of disciples were gathered there, and Jesus told them, "All authority in heaven and on earth has been given to Me." That means Jesus controls everything that happens on this earth—even when it looks like the devil is in control.

Jesus went on: "Go therefore and make disciples of all nations, baptizing them in the name of the Father and of the Son and of the Holy Spirit, teaching them to observe all that I have commanded you." This is the great mission Jesus gave to us, His Church. We are to tell the world, our neighbors, our family, and our friends about His great love—how He took our sins upon Himself and suffered and died on the cross in our place. We are to tell them He rose from the dead on the third day to destroy the power of death.

If that sounds like a hard thing to do, don't worry. Jesus added a great promise: "And behold, I am with you always, to the end of the age" (Matthew 28:20). Wherever we go, whatever we do, Jesus will always be there to help us, keep us safe in faith, and give us everything we need.

Finally, forty days after He rose from the dead, Jesus gathered His disciples in Jerusalem again. He told them they would be His witnesses. They would tell people about His life, His words, and His mighty miracles. They would tell about His suffering and death on the cross that took away all their sins, and about His powerful resurrection on Easter that gave them eternal life.

Jesus walked with them to Bethany. Then, while He was talking with them, He suddenly started to rise up off the ground. While they watched, He rose higher and higher into the air until He went up through the clouds and left them. He entered heaven and sat down at the right hand of God His Father. Now, He prays for us and rules everything that happens in the whole world for the good of His Church. He will be at the Father's right hand until Judgment Day comes. Then, He will come back down from heaven with all His angels to judge the world.

If you have grandparents or an aunt or uncle who lives far away, you know how sad it can be when they have to leave you or you have to leave them after a visit. It might seem sad that Jesus rose up—ascended—into heaven, but that doesn't mean He left us. Jesus is always here with us, living in our hearts, speaking to us through the Bible, forgiving our sins, and protecting and guiding us.

LET'S PRAY: Lord Jesus, thank You for ruling everything for the good of Your Church. Give us courage and boldness to tell everyone Your great story. Amen.

Pentecost

What languages do you know? Which would you like to learn?

After Jesus ascended into heaven, His disciples went back into Jerusalem. When they were gathered together, Peter told them someone needed to take Judas's place as one of the twelve apostles. They considered two men who had been with Jesus from His Baptism until His ascension. After they prayed, Matthias was chosen as the new disciple.

Ten days after Jesus ascended into heaven, there was an old Jewish festival in Jerusalem called Pentecost (PEN-tih-kawst). God had first told Moses about the Festival of Pentecost when they met together on Mount Sinai. Pentecost celebrated the first harvest of the year, when food was gathered and brought in from the fields. Jews came to Jerusalem from all over the world for Pentecost, thus there were many different languages spoken.

On this Pentecost Sunday, Jesus' disciples were gathered together in one place. Suddenly, a loud sound like a fast-blowing wind came from heaven and filled the house where they were. The disciples saw what looked like tongues of fire spread out and rest on everyone. All the people there began speaking in a language they had never studied or learned before. The Holy Spirit gave them power to understand and speak different languages!

Many of the Jews who were gathered in Jerusalem for Pentecost heard the sound and rushed over to see what was going on. Suddenly, they heard the disciples speaking the Good News about Jesus in their own languages they had spoken since they were children.

But some of the Jews who lived in Jerusalem made fun of the disciples and said they were drunk.

When Peter heard this, he got everyone's attention and raised his voice to speak to them.

He explained that the disciples were not drunk, but that God had poured out the Holy Spirit, who gave them the ability to speak in the different languages of the Jews gathered together in Jerusalem.

Peter told them this was exactly what the Old Testament prophet Joel had said would happen in the last days when God poured out His Spirit. Then, Peter explained why it had happened: because God had sent Jesus Christ, His Son, the promised Savior to them. Instead of believing in Him, however, they had rejected Him and killed Him on the cross, but God had raised Him from the dead. The disciples had seen Jesus many times after He had risen from the dead, and now they were urging every Jew who heard them to be baptized. That day, three thousand Jews became disciples of Jesus and members of the Church.

Today, the Bible has been written down in many different languages so people all around the world can know how Jesus came to save them. The Holy Spirit came to us at our Baptism to give us faith in Jesus and to keep that faith strong. He gives us courage to tell other people about Jesus and works to give them faith when they hear.

LET'S PRAY: Heavenly Father, thank You for sending us Your Holy Spirit so we are able to believe in Jesus as our Lord and Savior. Give us boldness from the Holy Spirit so we are never afraid to share the Good News of Jesus. Amen.

Peter and John Heal a Man Who Can't Walk

Acts 3

What would you say to someone who doesn't care about Jesus?

One day, Peter and John passed a beggar on their way to the temple. This man's legs were so weak he had never in his whole life been able to walk. At that time, if you couldn't walk, then you couldn't work, so the man begged for money, hoping the people who passed by would feel sorry for him and give him some.

When he saw Peter and John, he asked them for some money. Peter told him, "Look at us." The man looked closely at them, expecting some money. Peter told him, "I have no silver and gold, but what I do have I give to you. In the name of Jesus Christ of Nazareth, rise up and walk!" Peter grabbed his right hand and helped him to his feet.

Immediately, the man felt his feet and ankles grow strong, and he leaped up and began walking around. He followed Peter and John into the temple. The people in the temple recognized the beggar and were amazed to see him jumping and leaping. They rushed in to take a closer look.

Peter asked them, "Men of Israel, why do you wonder at this?" He told them the God of their fathers Abraham, Isaac, and Jacob had given Jesus glory, but they had handed Him over to Pilate to be killed. They had denied Jesus, the promised Messiah, and had asked Pilate to release the murderer Barabbas instead of Jesus. They had killed the Son of God, who had created all life. But God had raised Jesus from the dead, and Peter and John and all the apostles were witnesses who had seen Him alive. Peter told them Jesus had healed the beggar and made him strong.

Peter told the people they had not known what they were doing when they had crucified Jesus, but now was the time to be sorry for what they had done and ask God to forgive them for Jesus' sake.

The Jewish priests did not like what Peter and John were saying, and they sent guards to arrest them and put them in jail for the night. The next morning, the Jewish leaders met, but they couldn't do anything because everyone in Jerusalem knew the man, and it was clear that he had been healed. So all they could do was warn Peter and John to stop talking about Jesus.

Peter told the priests they had to decide for themselves what was right and wrong. But Peter, John, and Jesus' other apostles had to do what God sent them to do.

Some people don't like us to talk about Jesus. But Jesus commanded us to tell everyone He loves them and wants to save them. We won't be rude and pushy; we won't make them talk about God if they don't want to. But we will pray for Jesus to show us the right time to talk and ask Him to help us speak boldly when that time comes.

> **LET'S PRAY:** Holy Father, thank You for giving Peter and John healing power so the people at the temple were ready to listen closely to what Peter told them. Give me courage to speak, and make other people ready to listen to the Good News about Jesus, their Savior. Amen.

Stephen, the First Christian to Die

Acts 6–7

Why is it so hard to be nice to someone who has hurt you?

As the twelve apostles taught about Jesus in the temple, many Jews believed and were baptized. The Early Church started to grow very quickly. Among the Christians, there were many widows, women whose husbands had died and didn't have money to take care of themselves. The Christians took up offerings to buy food for them.

The problem was that the widows from Jerusalem were getting taken care of, but not the widows from far away. When the apostles learned about it, they were concerned. They wanted to make sure everyone who needed help got taken care of, but Jesus had sent them to preach the Good News, not to serve tables. They said, "Brothers, pick out seven men who are full of the Spirit and of wisdom, whom we will appoint to this duty." These men would make sure every person got help. One of those seven men was named Stephen.

Stephen was full of grace and power by the Holy Spirit. He did great miracles, just like the apostles were doing. When some Jews who didn't believe in Jesus started arguing with him, the Holy Spirit made Stephen so wise he proved they were wrong. Sadly, they didn't believe Stephen. They just got more angry with him.

They took Stephen to the high priest, Caiaphas, and also to the same Jewish court that had decided to put Jesus to death. The Jewish court looked at Stephen and noticed his face was like an angel's face, probably glowing.

The Holy Spirit made Stephen very, very wise. Stephen told the Jewish leaders about all the times in the Old Testament when God had raised up a leader for His people Israel but the Israelites had refused to follow him. He talked about leaders like Joseph, Moses, and King David—and how the Israelites had grumbled against them and refused to obey them. And now, when God had sent His own promised Son, they had done even worse to Him—they had betrayed and murdered Jesus.

When the priests and other leaders heard this, they got so mad they put their fingers in their ears, rushed together at Stephen, dragged him outside, and picked up big stones and rocks to throw at him and kill him.

As Stephen was being stoned, he prayed to Jesus, "Lord Jesus, receive my spirit." He said, "Lord, do not hold this sin against them." Then Stephen died, and his spirit went to heaven.

One of the hardest things for us to do is to forgive people who are hurting us—especially if they do it because we believe in Jesus. But the Holy Spirit made Stephen strong, and He can make you strong to pray for those who hurt you and to boldly tell everyone the Good News of what Jesus did to save us all.

LET'S PRAY: Lord Jesus, thank You for giving the Holy Spirit to make Stephen so bold and strong. Give me Your Holy Spirit too, so I can have the courage to tell others about You, especially when people want to hurt me for believing in You. Amen.

The Conversion of Saul

Acts 9:1–31

What would you do if someone who had always been really mean to you suddenly wanted to be your friend?

Earlier in Acts, a Christian named Stephen, who told the Good News about Jesus, was killed by the Jewish leaders, who threw big stones and rocks at him. As they got ready to throw the stones, the Jewish leaders took off their coats and laid them at the feet of a young man named Saul, who also thought Stephen should die for believing in Jesus.

Saul believed Jesus was a false teacher who taught lies about God and pretended to be God's Son. He wanted to stop the Christians from telling other people about Jesus, so he went from house to house through Jerusalem, dragging off the people who believed in Jesus and putting them in prison.

Saul wanted to attack the Christians in Damascus, so the high priest wrote letters for him so that if he found any believers in Jesus, he could tie them up and bring them back to Jerusalem.

When Saul came near Damascus, "suddenly a light from heaven shone around him." He fell to the ground and heard a voice calling, "Saul, Saul, why are you persecuting Me?" Saul asked, "Who are You, Lord?" The voice answered, "I am Jesus, whom you are persecuting. But rise and enter the city, and you will be told what you are to do."

The men traveling with Saul heard the voice, but they didn't see anyone. Saul got up off the ground, but when he opened his eyes he couldn't see anything. The men took his hand and led him into Damascus. For three days, Saul was unable to see. He didn't eat or drink anything during this time.

Then, Jesus told a Christian in Damascus named Ananias (an-uh-NIGH-uhs) to go and lay his hands on Saul so he could see again. Ananias was scared of Saul, but he obeyed Jesus. He went and laid his hands on Saul, and Jesus gave Saul back his sight. Ananias baptized him.

Right there in Damascus, Saul began teaching that Jesus was the Christ, the Savior of the world. Some Jews got angry and made plans to kill Saul. But Saul found out and had his disciples lower him down in a basket through an opening in the wall.

Saul returned to Jerusalem, but the Christians there were afraid of him. A devout Christian named Barnabas took Saul to the apostles and described how Jesus had appeared to Saul on the road to Damascus. The apostles welcomed Saul, and he became known as Paul.

Sometimes, people do very bad things that hurt us. Even if they start being nice, we don't know if we can trust them or not. But Jesus loves them just like He loves us. And He can change them so they can work hard for their Savior and for all of us Christians.

LET'S PRAY: Lord Jesus, thank You for loving Saul, even though he did horrible things to Your people. Remind me that You suffered and died for all people—even those who treat me very badly. Help me to forgive them and pray for them, that they may believe You are their Savior too. Amen.

Peter Is Freed from Prison

When bad and scary things happen to you, where do you think God is?

While Paul began sharing his new faith, Peter and the other apostles continued to boldly tell people the Good News about Jesus. That's when a new King Herod decided to attack the Church. His grandfather was King Herod the Great, the king who tried to kill little Jesus after the Wise Men came. His uncle was Herod Antipas, who killed John the Baptist.

Like the other Herods, this one wanted the Jewish rulers to like him, so he arrested John's brother James and had him killed. That made James the first of the twelve apostles to die for Jesus. When Herod learned he had made the Jewish leaders happy by killing James, he arrested Peter and announced he would bring him out and kill him after the Passover. Many Christians heard the terrible news, gathered together, and spent the night praying for Jesus to save Peter.

Late that night, Peter was in jail sleeping between two guards, who were both chained to him. Suddenly, in the middle of the night, an angel appeared in Peter's cell, and a light shone around him. The angel struck Peter on the side and said, "Get up quickly." When he got up, the chains fell off his hands. The angel told Peter to get dressed and follow him. At first, Peter didn't think this was actually happening; he thought Jesus was giving him a vision.

The angel led him past the first guard and the second. When they came near the iron gate that led into the city, it opened by itself. The angel led him along one street and then immediately left him. That's when Peter realized Jesus had really set him free.

He went to the house where the Christians were praying for him, and he knocked on the door. A servant girl named Rhoda recognized his voice. She was so excited that she left him outside while she ran in to tell the others that Peter was there. At first they told her, "You are out of your mind." But then they heard Peter knocking at the door. They opened it, saw Peter, and were amazed. He waved his hand to quiet them down; then, he told them how God had saved him. He said, "Tell these things to James and to the brothers." This James was the brother of Jesus, the leader of the Church in Jerusalem. Then, Peter left to go to another city where he could safely teach people about Jesus.

God always watches over us—even when bad things happen to us. Though King Herod killed James, Jesus had promised James that He would raise him from the grave at the Last Day. He set Peter free so he could keep telling the Good News about Jesus. You can trust God to watch over you and never let anything keep you out of His home in heaven.

LET'S PRAY: Lord Jesus, thank You for taking James home to heaven and protecting Peter so he could stay and tell Your story to people who needed to hear it. Give me faith to trust You and courage to share the Good News of Your love wherever I am. Amen.

Paul's First Missionary Journey

Describe a time you were asked to do something important.

While Peter went from place to place sharing the Good News about Jesus, Paul and Barnabas were living in a town called Antioch. They met some very fine and strong Christians there. One time while the people in the Antioch church were praying, the Holy Spirit told them, "Set apart for Me Barnabas and Saul [Paul] for the work to which I have called them." The Christians prayed and laid their hands on the heads of Barnabas and Paul. Then, the Holy Spirit sent them off to go and visit new places and tell the people there about Jesus' life, death, and resurrection.

You might remember that when the Holy Spirit came at Pentecost, Jerusalem was filled with Jews who had gathered in town from all over the world for the feast. Instead of keeping His Church in Jerusalem, God was now sending believers out into the world with the Good News of Jesus. They left the land of Israel, and the Church grew bigger and began to spread out into the world.

Every time Paul and Barnabas entered a new city, they looked for Jews and their synagogues. That's because Jews were spread out all over the Roman Empire. Barnabas and Paul could find a synagoguc in most of the towns they went to. That is where they started. They went to the synagogue on the Sabbath Day, Saturday, and taught the Jews there about Jesus. Then, on the other days of the week, they talked about Jesus to everyone they met, Jews and Gentiles.

They were doing the same thing Jesus had done when He went preaching throughout the land of Israel. Whenever He entered a town or village, He went to the services at the synagogues on the Sabbath and taught them about God's kingdom. Then, during the week, He visited and talked with people wherever He met them: on the streets, at wells, in the marketplaces, or in people's houses.

As Barnabas and Paul shared the faith in the towns where they traveled, the Jews and Gentiles who believed in Jesus gathered together and started to form churches. God was with them, and in the cities where they traveled, many people came to believe. Barnabas and Paul picked leaders who were strong believers, taught them to be pastors, and put them in charge of the congregations while they moved on to the next town.

God may not call you to be a missionary, leave your country, and go to live in distant places teaching people about Jesus, but He might. He may not call you to be a pastor or a teacher in some other part of our country, but He might. But even if God doesn't call you to be a missionary, pastor, or teacher, He does send you to your classmates, friends, neighbors, and even people you don't know so you can tell them about Jesus and how He loves them and died for them. The Holy Spirit will guide you and teach you exactly what to say.

LET'S PRAY: Lord Jesus, thank You for making Barnabas and Paul's missionary journeys so successful. Help me tell my friends and others about You so they might also believe and learn how great You are. Amen.

Paul and Silas in Prison

Acts 16:16–40

Have you ever gotten in trouble for doing something nice?

Paul finished his first missionary journey with Barnabas; then, he told his friend they should go back and see how the new churches were doing. Barnabas liked the idea and wanted to take along his cousin Mark (who later wrote the Gospel of Mark). But Paul didn't think that was a good idea.

Mark had gone with them on their first missionary journey, but right in the middle he had left to go back home, even though Barnabas and Paul still needed him. Paul didn't want that to happen again. Barnabas said it wouldn't, but Paul didn't want to take the chance. Since they couldn't agree, they split up to go to different places. Paul brought along his friend Silas, while Barnabas took Mark along with him to a different place.

Paul and Silas came to a city called Philippi (fih-LIPP-eye). They talked to a group of people, and the Holy Spirit created faith in a wealthy woman named Lydia. She welcomed them to stay in her house.

As Paul and Silas shared the Gospel in the city, a slave girl who had a demon followed them around, saying, "These men are servants of the Most High God, who proclaim to you the way of salvation." Paul turned and said to the demon, "I command you in the name of Jesus Christ to come out of her." And the demon immediately left her.

That made the people mad who owned the slave girl. Back when she still had the demon, they had earned a lot of money from others who wanted her to tell their futures. But now with the demon gone, their chance to make a lot of money was gone. They grabbed Paul and Silas and dragged them before the judges.

The judges ordered that they be beaten with rods and put in prison for the night. But Paul and Silas didn't sit around feeling sorry for themselves. Around midnight, they were praying and singing in their prison cell, and all the other prisoners were listening. Suddenly, a strong earthquake struck, and all the prison doors opened up and the chains fell off of every prisoner.

The jailer who was in charge of the prison woke up and got really scared. He saw the jail doors standing open and thought all the prisoners had escaped. Since he thought that he had failed to keep them in jail, he pulled out his sword to kill himself. But Paul shouted that he should not hurt himself, because all the prisoners were still there. The jailer asked for a torch and ran inside to see. He fell down in front of Paul and Silas and asked what he had to do to be saved. Paul told him, "Believe in the Lord Jesus, and you will be saved, you and your household." Then, Paul and Silas told the jailer and his family and servants all about Jesus. They baptized his whole household.

Sometimes, we try to be nice to people but they treat us very badly. That may make you want to stop being nice and telling people about Jesus. But remember Paul and Silas. Pray to Jesus and sing hymns to say thanks to Him. He will take away your sorrow and fill you with His joy. The Holy Spirit will show you how you can teach someone about Jesus.

LET'S PRAY: Lord Jesus, thank You for the bold faith of Paul and Silas. Give me such thankfulness and courage that people will want to know all about You. Amen.

Name someplace you wanted to go or something you wanted to do but couldn't.

After Paul and Silas were freed from prison and finished the second missionary journey, they rested a bit. Then, they took a third journey that ended in Jerusalem. On this journey, they preached the Gospel and performed miracles in Jesus' name, such as when Jesus raised a young man named Eutychus (YOO-tih-kuhs) from the dead through Paul (see Acts 20:7–12). In each city, they found Jews and Gentiles who were glad to hear the Good News about Jesus, but there were also many who tried to make them stop.

While Paul was at the temple in Jerusalem, he was spotted by some of the Jews who had tried to stop him during his missionary journeys. They cried for help, telling the Jews of Jerusalem that Paul was bringing Gentiles into the temple against God's Law. They grabbed Paul and started beating him—even though no Gentiles were in the temple with him.

Then, soldiers from the Roman army marched in, grabbed Paul, and took him to safety. Since some Jews made plans to attack and kill him in Jerusalem, the Roman soldiers took him out of town at night on horseback and led him to a safe place called Caesarea (sez-uh-REE-uh).

Paul had wanted to go on and travel to new parts of the Roman Empire to share the Good News about Jesus, but he had to stay under guard in Caesarea for two years until the new governor, Festus, came. Festus planned to take Paul to Jerusalem for his trial, but Paul knew the Jews there were planning to kill him. So he asked to have his trial before the Roman Emperor, and Paul was put on a ship to sail across the sea to Rome.

Along the way, a strong storm came up that lasted for two whole weeks! Finally, on the fourteenth day, they saw an island beach and tried to sail the ship there, but it struck ground and the powerful waves tore it into pieces. Everyone jumped into the water and made it safely to shore.

But they were all wet, and the night was cold and rainy. The island people started a big fire to warm the travelers. As Paul was gathering sticks, a snake came out and bit him on the hand. The island people thought God was punishing Paul and watched for him to die from the snakebite. But Paul's hand did not swell up, and he didn't fall over and die. So the people thought he must be a god instead. The chief man on the island welcomed Paul to his house, and Paul healed the man's father, who was sick with a fever. After that, sick people from the island came, and Jesus healed all of them through Paul. The journey and shipwreck gave Paul the chance to share the story of Jesus with the soldiers, the sailors, and now the people from the island.

Like Paul, we sometimes find that life doesn't go the way we want it to, and we go through hard times. But Jesus promises He will always be with us, no matter what happens. He will even use the hard times in our lives to reach other people with the Good News, and He will guide us safely to live with Him in heaven.

LET'S PRAY: Lord Jesus, You watched carefully over Paul and everyone with him on that boat. Help me know You will always be with me so I will never need to be afraid. Amen.

What things make you bold and strong when you get discouraged?

Peter and Paul spent their last days in Rome, and some say that both were put to death on the same day. All but one of Jesus' twelve apostles were put to death for their faith in Jesus. The last of the Twelve was John, the brother of James, who took care of Mary after Jesus died.

John wasn't put to death, but he was exiled. He was forced to leave his people and live on an island called Patmos (PAT-mahs). For an apostle, being away from Christians was one of the hardest things.

But something very important happened while John was in exile. Jesus showed him a revelation that God the Father had given Him. It showed John what was happening in heaven and on earth.

That is so important because sometimes really bad things happen. Sometimes, it feels like Jesus doesn't know what's happening to us or He doesn't care about us. Jesus gave John this revelation to write down so we could remember that God is in control of everything that happens in this world, and one day He will come again to take away all the bad things and make His creation new, perfect, and wonderful forever—and that includes each of us believers too.

In the revelation, John saw Jesus in heaven. He wrote about it: "I saw . . . one like a son of man. . . . The hairs of His head were white, like white wool, like snow. His eyes were like a flame of fire, His feet were like burnished bronze, refined in a furnace, and His voice was like the roar of many waters. . . . His face was like the sun shining in full strength" (Revelation 1:12–16).

John was very scared when he saw the glory of Jesus, the Son of God. He fell at our Savior's feet like he was dead. But Jesus laid His hand on John and told him not to be afraid: "Fear not, I am the first and the last, and the living one. I died, and behold I am alive forevermore. . . . Write therefore the things that you have seen, those that are and those that are to take place after this" (Revelation 1:17–19).

So John wrote it all down in what became the last book of the Bible, Revelation. It tells us that God supervises all things and orders events so unbelievers will repent and glorify Him.

John finished his Book of Revelation with a promise from Jesus: "Surely I am coming soon." John's answer is our prayer, "Amen. Come, Lord Jesus!" (Revelation 22:20).

During this life, you will have good times and bad, happy times and sad. But Jesus will never leave you. He will guard and protect you, and on the Last Day He will come back to punish Satan and all his demons. But for us who love Jesus and look forward to His return, He will make us shine like the stars in heaven and give us a new heaven and a new earth.

LET'S PRAY: Lord Jesus, thank You for coming the first time at Bethlehem to save us, for coming today to teach us with Your words, and for Your promise to come on the Last Day to make this earth new and perfect forever. Keep me in this faith until You return. Amen.